The politics of transport

POLITICS TODAY

General Editors: *Bernard Crick, Patrick Seyd*

POLITICAL ISSUES IN MODERN BRITAIN
Published by Fontana

THE POLITICS OF TRANSPORT

Enid Wistrich

LONGMAN
London and New York

LONGMAN GROUP LIMITED
Longman House, Burnt Mill, Harlow
Essex CM20 2JE, England
Associated companies throughout the world

*Published in the United States of America
by Longman Inc., New York*

First published 1983

BRITISH LIBRARY CATALOGUING IN PUBLICATION DATA

Wistrich, Enid
   The politics of transport. — (Politics today)
   1. Transportation — Political aspects
   I. Title   II. Series
   380.5   HE141
   ISBN 0-582-29523-8

LIBRARY OF CONGRESS CATALOGING IN PUBLICATION DATA

Wistrich, Enid.
   The politics of transport.

   (Politics today)
   Bibliography: p.
   Includes index.
   1. Transportation and state — Great Britain.
2. Transportation planning — Great Britain. I. Title.
II. Series.
HE243.A1W57   1983   380.5'068   82-17923
ISBN 0-582-29523-8

Set in 10/11 pt Linotron 202 Plantin
Printed in Hong Kong
by Astros Printing Ltd

CONTENTS

EDITORS' PREFACE

There is a demand among the general public as well as from students for books that deal with the main issues of modern British politics in such a way that the reader can gain a reliable account of how an issue arose, of its institutional context and then, but only then, to have argument about what should be done.

Behind what have become political issues, there are fundamental problems. Many books identify these problems theoretically, but too often ignore the empirical context, and others are so polemical and doctrinaire, that their conclusions, however just, are distrusted by shrewd readers. We believe in casting out neither facts nor values, but in relating them closely but distinctly. The test of a good book on political issues should be that a reader will feel that he has a full and reliable account of how the issue arose and what institutions and groups affect and are affected by it, irrespective of what the author thinks should be done. But authors cannot just describe, inevitably they prescribe; so let it be done openly and clearly. Politics is too important for neutrality, but therefore demanding of objectivity. So we ask the authors in this series to organise the books into three parts: the recent history of the matter, the institutional setting, and argument about the future.

We believe that relevant books are wanted, neither wholly committed books nor those that pretend to scientific objectivity. This series continues work that we began with Fontana Books, in their 'Political Issues' series. Some similarities will be obvious, particularly in our injunction to authors to write at the highest possible level of intelligence but to eschew all jargon and technicalities. Students of politics should accept, not worry, that they have a public role.

Bernard Crick and Patrick Seyd

AUTHOR'S PREFACE

Transport has many facets and is the subject of study and analysis by several professions and academic disciplines. In attempting to provide an overview of recent events, issues and ideas, I am conscious of the problem of doing justice to the many people and professions who have contributed to their development. Except for Chapter 3, which is a summary of developments in the transport systems, I have concentrated on the longer-term trends and patterns of behaviour and on the controversial issues.

My thanks are due to the people and organizations who supplied me with information, and my apologies to them for not having the space to give as full account as I would have liked of their work. They include Douglas Jay MP, William Rodgers MP, Roger Liddle, Michael Harris, Nick Lester, Jonathan Roberts, Tony Howell, John Fitzpatrick and other officers of the GLC, Gillian Courtenay, Richard Fleming, David Wiggins, Tony Smith, Stephen Potter and the officers of the organizations referred to in the book.

Bernard Crick read the first draft and gave invaluable strategic advice which guided the shape of the second one. Peggy Gentry typed both with great skill and good humour. Ernest Wistrich bore the brunt of my peevish preoccupation with equanimity and developed a useful knowledge of the best take-away food shops in our area. My friends learned to be careful about making cheerful enquiries as to when was I going to finish? I am very grateful to them all for their help and forbearance. I would also like to thank my employers at the Middlesex Polytechnic for allotting a research allowance on my timetable which made it more possible to find time to do the work.

Enid Wistrich

LIST OF ABBREVIATIONS

APT	Advanced Passenger Train
ASLEF	Associated Society of Locomotive Engineers and Firemen
AA	Automobile Association
BAPA	British Airline Pilots' Association
BAA	British Airports Authority
BA	British Airways
BEA	British European Airways
BOAC	British Overseas Airways Corporation
BRF	British Road Federation
BTC	British Transport Commission
CTCC	Central Transport Consultative Committee
CBI	Confederation of British Industry
CoEnCo	Council for Environmental Conservation
CPRE	Council for the Protection of Rural England
FTA	Freight Transport Association
GLC	Greater London Council
GLDP	Greater London Development Plan
IWA	Inland Waterways Association
LATA	London Amenity and Transport Association
LCC	London County Council
LMAG	London Motorway Action Group
NCC	National Consumers' Council
NCIT	National Council on Inland Transport
NEDO	National Economic Development Office
NUR	National Union of Railwaymen
PTE	Passenger Transport Executive
PTP	Passenger Transport Plan
PSO	Public Service Obligation
RIA	Railway Industry Association

RCU	Road Construction Unit
RHA	Road Haulage Association
RAC	Royal Automobile Club
SMMT	Society of Motor Manufacturers and Traders
TUC	Trades Union Congress
TGWU	Transport and General Workers' Union
TRRL	Transport and Road Research Laboratory
TPP	Transport Policies and Programme
TSSA	Transport Salaried Staffs' Association
TSG	Transport Supplementary Grant
TUCC	Transport Users' Consultative Committee
WARA	Wing Airport Resistance Association

ACKNOWLEDGEMENTS

We are indebted to Transport 2000 Ltd for permission to reproduce extracts from the 'Peeler Memorandum' published as a broadsheet by *Transport 2000* (1978).

Part one
DEVELOPMENTS AND CONTEXT SINCE 1945

Chapter one
TRENDS AND CONSEQUENCES

The full impact of the twentieth-century revolution in transport was not felt in Britain until the 1950s. The shift from rail to road as a means of transporting both goods and passengers exploded with sudden and unexpected vehemence after the artificial pause in its progress during the Second World War. The effects reverberated through the economy, the pattern of personal habits and expenditure and on the physical environment throughout the 1960s and 1970s and was reflected in the activity of pressure groups and political conflicts. By 1983 we have begun to understand what the implications are in terms of employment, industry, planning and public expenditure, though it is by no means clear what are the best public policies to manage the complex issues involved. Personal choices dictate the provision which is made, but equally are limited by it. The individual who can trade-off car against bus and train will argue for more road crossings as a pedestrian, for less congestion and free flow of traffic as a car driver and for more buses and cheaper fares on trains as a public transport user. The 'juggernaut' lorry is reviled and passionate pleas for convenient corner shops within walking distance are made by the same people who drive to the supermarket for a regular weekly haul of cheaply priced goods. Those without cars are steadily further disadvantaged. The contradictions are many, but the turmoil is dictated by the continuing degree of change in transport provision, the choices which are opened up for some and the limitations which also follow for others. To understand the turbulence of the politics of transport in the late twentieth century, it is necessary to appreciate the changes which have occurred and some of the effects they have had on peoples' living patterns.

The impact of the private car on opportunities, personal expenditure and living patterns is certainly comparable to the impact of

railway use during the nineteenth century. The railways made possible daily journeys to work beyond walking distance, shopping
expeditions to nearby towns and annual holidays by the sea for the
majority of the population who had never previously had those
opportunities. Car ownership brought a degree of mobility which
has affected a growing number of people as significantly in the
twentieth century. The change can be illustrated by reference to the
shift in official attitudes. Towards the end of the First World War,
a select committee considering what articles should be subject to
a duty to be imposed on luxuries decided that motor cars should
be included. By 1932, that official stigma was removed in the
Report of the Royal Commission on Transport which declared that
'private cars are not, as a class, articles of luxury'. Since 1945, successive governments and ministers have taken for granted the
spread of car ownership and have applauded it. Tony Crosland,
writing in 1956, spoke generally of 'social justice, which surely
requires that the masses, for so long deprived of luxuries which
others have enjoyed, should now also be admitted to the world of
material ease . . .', and again, 'we want to see individuals happy,
and rich, and enjoying what in the past have been solely the luxuries of the upper classes; and in the process we should take a long
stride towards the classless society' (Crosland 1956: 292, 294). The
Buchanan Report *Traffic in Towns* (1963) thought that 'as a longer
term objective, it is questionable whether anything is so much
desired as a family car'. By 1977 the Transport Policy White Paper
pointed out that 'we have come to take personal mobility and ease
of access for granted, in a way quite unknown to previous generations' (Dept of Transport 1977), and in 1981 the Transport Committee of the House of Commons asserted that 'whatever its
disadvantages . . . the invention of the internal combustion engine
has made a significant contribution to the development of our civi-
lisation and has given Western man a degree of personal mobility
which most clearly regard as a boon. The growth of private car
ownership has brought benefit to the majority of our citizens and
reflects the clear majority preference for a high degree of personal
mobility' (H of C 1981: vol. 1, para. 9).

The pattern of benefits arising from car ownership is not, however, evenly distributed. There are sections of the population who
benefit less and their needs are now less well met both comparatively and in many cases in absolute terms. They are also likely to
be the people who suffer disbenefit from the negative side-effects
of the developments. For example, pensioners and single-parent

3

families without a car on a low income will suffer from diminished public transport provision, limited availability of convenient shops for their needs, and poor conditions in their towns for pedestrians arising from greater traffic congestion. While significant gains have been obtained for a large section of the population, the benefits are not evenly spread either between social classes, areas of the country or even between different members of the same family.

These trends may be analysed by reference to the use of transport modes and of car ownership and use. The first point to note is the large absolute increase in the amount of passenger travel over the last twenty-five years. Between 1954 and 1980, the total distances travelled in Britain increased from 215 billion passenger km to 528. The overwhelming part of this increase came from journeys in private road vehicles which increased five-fold from 76 to 433 billion km. Journeys by air within the country increased as dramatically from 0.3 to 2.8 billion km but their contribution to the total was tiny. The increase in car and plane use was not only absolute but achieved at the expense of journeys by bus, train and pedal cycle, all of which declined in use in absolute terms over the period. The significance of the different modes may be seen in the percentage distribution of the modes according to journey distances (see Table 1.1). Private cars more than doubled their share from 35 per cent in 1954 to 76 per cent in 1970 and then more slowly to 82 per cent in 1980. The drop in bus and coach mileage as a proportion of the total was even more dramatic (from 38 to 10 per cent), and rail journeys which are well suited to longer-distance journeys dropped their share by over a half of the total from 18 to 7 per cent. If we compare the period 1960–70 with 1970–80, the growth in car travel appears to be slowing down. It more than doubled in the first ten years but increased by only three-quarters in the second. The fall in bus, train and pedal-cycle mileage also slowed down considerably. Whether the car travel explosion in terms of distances travelled is now easing up and the public transport systems are stabilizing their proportion of the market is a possibility which will be clarified over the next ten years.

The same trends can also be seen in the number of vehicles and the statistics of car ownership (see Table 1.2 and 1.3 (a)). The number of private cars and vans licensed roughly doubled in each of three ten-year periods from 1930–39, 1950–60 and 1960–70, but the growth was less than a third from 1970–80. Between 1961–70, the proportion of households with regular use of a car jumped from 31 to 52 per cent and by 1979 to 58 per cent. Car ownership which

Table 1.1 Passenger transport modes 1954–80

	1954		1960		1970		1980	
	(bill. km)	(%)	(bill. km)	(%)	(bill. km)	(%)	(bill. km)	(%)
Buses and coaches	81	38	71	27	56	14	51	10
Private road vehicles	76	35	144	54	309	76	433	82
Pedal cycles	19	9	12	5	5	1	5	1
All road	176	82	227	86	370	91	489	93
Rail	39	18	40	15	36	9	36	7
Air (within UK)	0.3	0.1	0.8	0.3	2.0	0.5	2.8	0.5
All modes	215	100	268	100	408	100	528	100

Source: Transport Statistics 1970–80, HMSO

Table 1.2   Numbers of motor vehicles licensed in Great Britain 1930–80

	Private cars and vans	*All vehicles*
1930	1,056	2,272
1939	2,034	3,149
1950	2,258	4,409
1960	5,526	9,439
1970	11,515	14,950
1980	15,073	19,210

Source: Transport Statistics 1970–80

rose from 0.17 per person in 1965 to 0.26 in 1978 is still projected to rise to between 0.37 and 0.42 per person by the end of the century. However, on the basis of experience in the last ten years, it is likely that a good deal of this growth will be in second and third cars within the same household. This tendency can be seen in the growth in cars per household between 1970–79, when the proportion of households with regular use of two or more cars increased from 8 to 13 per cent while the proportion using one car stayed steady at 44 per cent (see Table 1.3).

The link between car use and income level is clear from the analysis of car ownership by socio-economic group in 1980 and of the percentage of journeys made by car as the main mode of transport, analysed by household income level. For car ownership, the proportion of households without a car almost exactly matches the progression down the socio-economic scale, ending with 71 per cent for the unskilled manual group and 70 per cent for the economically inactive, while households with two or more cars go correspondingly in an opposite direction (see Table 1.3c). Looking at journeys, the proportion of car journeys to the total rises steadily from 16 per cent for the lowest incomes to 65 per cent for the top income level (see Table 1.4).

In the same analysis, local bus as a mode was highest for the lowest income and steadily diminished in importance, as did walking as a main transport mode. Train use, however, rose with income, reflecting income ability to make longer-distance, more expensive journeys.

The extent of car use is not even over the whole country. In the areas which we already identify as the regions of lower economic prosperity – Scotland and the North of England – in 1978 the proportion of households with no regular use of a car remained at

Table 1.3   Households with regular use of cars in Great Britain (%)

	No car	*One car*	*Two or more cars*
(a) Great Britain 1961–79			
1961	69	29	2
1970	48	44	8
1979	42	44	13
(b) Analysed by region 1978			
England – total	42	45	13
North	50	41	9
Yorkshire	50	41	9
North West	48	41	10
E. Midlands	40	47	13
W. Midlands	41	46	13
E. Anglia	34	51	15
South-East (excl. Greater London)	33	50	17
South-West	35	51	14
Greater London	47	42	10
Scotland	53	39	8
Wales	38	49	13
Great Britain – total	43	45	12
(c) Analysed by socio-economic group of head of household 1980 (car or van)			
Professional	9	55	36
Employers and managers	6	50	44
Intermediate non-manual	18	63	19
Junior non-manual	36	50	14
Skilled manual	25	59	16
Semi-skilled manual	49	43	8
Unskilled manual	71	27	2
All economically active	27	53	20
Economically inactive	70	26	3

Source: (a) and (b) *Transport Statistics 1970–78*
(c) *Social Trends, HMSO, 1982*

48–53 per cent (see Table 1.3(b)). Going further south, that proportion diminished through the Midlands (40–41%) and went down to 33 per cent in the South-East of England. In Greater London, it remained high at 47 per cent, possibly because of the large number of single-person households and the well-developed public transport

Table 1.4 Journeys by different modes analysed by household income
1975–76

	Main mode of transport, % of journeys					
Household income (£)	Train	Local bus	Other public transport	Private car/van	Walking	Motor & pedal cycle & other
Nil	5	18	2	27	45	3
Up to 749	1	23	2	16	55	2
750–1,249	1	22	2	21	50	5
1,250–1,499	1	16	3	29	47	5
1,500–1,999	1	16	2	31	45	6
2,000–2,499	1	13	2	37	43	4
2,500–2,999	1	12	2	40	40	5
3,000–3,999	1	11	2	44	37	4
4,000–4,999	2	9	2	50	33	4
5,000–5,999	2	10	2	50	31	4
6,000–7,499	3	9	2	54	29	4
7,500–9,999	2	7	2	62	24	4
Over 10,000	4	4	1	65	21	4

Source: National Travel Survey 1975, Hamer and Potter, (1979)

system. Wales showed a low proportion at 38 per cent. The figures
matched at the other end of the spectrum too where the proportion
of households with two or more cars reached 17 per cent in South-
East England but fell to 8 per cent in Scotland.

The match between car use and region is not solely a function
of income. Access to facilities is another important factor which
cuts across income groups. Thus, a more detailed analysis of car
ownership made for the National Travel Survey of 1975/76 showed
that car ownership was higher for lower-income households in areas
of low population density than in areas of high population density
(Hillman and Whalley 1979). The propensity of higher-income
households to own a second car rose steadily as the population density dropped. The percentage of women holding driving licences
also rose steadily as population density decreased. Clearly the lack
of facilities close by in country regions makes households more
willing to own and use cars than in towns where shops, schools and
hospitals are more likely to be within walking distance.

A description of the overall car use for households does not, however, complete the picture. The access to car use varies for different members of every household. In the first place, the person who does not drive is dependent on the licence holder as an escort. Secondly, if one person uses a household's single car for the journey to work, the car goes out of use for the rest of the household for all weekday daytime hours. The other people in one-car owning households (45% of the total) may well be without access to the household's car for most of the week and in a comparable position to the 43 per cent of households without any car. Other evidence indicates that the main car users are the men in a household. To start with, they predominate as car drivers: 64 per cent of all driving licences were held by men in 1979. An analysis in the National Travel Survey 1975–76 of the percentage of journeys made by men and women of working age for different purposes showed that men used cars more than women not only for journeys to work (64% against 36%) but also for most other types of journey such as shopping (53% against 31%), and journeys for social purposes (65% against 52%) (Hamer and Potter 1979). Women rely more on walking and public transport for all types of journeys. The same survey figures show that teenagers and pensioners are more dependent on public transport for travel than men and women of working age.

It is also useful to retain an accurate sense of the proportions of all journeys by different modes and not to neglect the short journeys made on foot. If journeys include those under one mile, walking jumps to 35 per cent of the total, compared with 40 per cent by car, and 11 per cent by public transport. Walking is the most important mode for children and pensioners who make 51 and 46 per cent of all their journeys on foot. The proportions drop to 37 per cent for women of working age and 21 per cent for men. The information on walking also shows that it decreases as household income and car ownership rises.

The picture which emerges is therefore a complex one. The most consistent beneficiary from car use is the man of working age of a higher income level living in the southern area of Britain. The most dependent users of public transport are women and teenagers. Men of working age are less inclined to walk for any purpose than women, teenagers, children and pensioners of both sexes. Lower-income households will be more likely to own a car in an area of sparse population than in a town. The spread of car ownership is likely to continue, and especially the ownership of second and third cars, most markedly in areas of sparser population.

Overall, there has been an increase in the proportion of their income which people spend on transport and on their vehicles. From 9 per cent in 1961, it has increased to 12 per cent in 1970 and 14 per cent in 1979 (*Social Trends* 1979). And the higher the income, the higher the proportion spent. By and large, greater personal mobility, as reflected in expenditure on transport, appears to be a function of income.

Increasingly, provision of many kinds of facilities is made for car-owning households. In the case of shopping centres, for example, where the retailers gain from larger units, the tendency has been to provide centres away from the traditional town centres and high streets, sometimes located in 'green field' or other vacant sites at some distance from residential areas. In one such site on the outskirts of London, a study of the clientele of the thriving centre drawing on a regional catchment found that 74 per cent of the clientele were from households which owned cars, 41 per cent were in the professional, managerial or employer economic groups, only 16 per cent were over 60 years old, and their median gross weekly income was nearly twice that of people who did not shop at the centre (GLC 1980). Although adequate bus services were provided to the centre, the journey cost and time involved made it less attractive to the poorer and older sections of the population compared with local shops. The increased mobility of car ownership in this instance brought the advantage of access to an enhanced choice of shopping facilities; correspondingly, the carless population were relatively disadvantaged.

The shift in passenger transport from rail to road is matched by the shift in freight transport. The total distances that freight is carried has nearly doubled in the last twenty-five years. The tonnage carried by road is now nearly nine times the amount which goes by rail. Although rail clearly has advantages for longer-distance hauls, it was responsible for only 13 per cent of all ton mileage in 1979 and has lost a quarter of its share of the total since 1953.

The shift to road transport has not meant a comparable increase in the number of goods vehicles. The total of all goods vehicles rose from 1.3 m. in 1960 to 1.7 m. in 1979 but the number of lorries over 1.5 tons actually dropped from 585,000 to 544,000 (see Table 1.6). The decrease has, however, been in the middle-size range of lorries, between 1.5 and 5 tons in unladen weight. Lorries over 5 tons in weight have jumped in numbers from 52,000 in 1960 to 235,000 in 1979. The image of the 'juggernaut' is not a fiction: there are now 121,000 eight tonners working in Britain. And even if the numbers of lorries have diminished in relation to the total of motor

Table 1.5 Goods transported by mode of transport

	1953		1979		1959		1979	
	Million tons	%	Million tons	%	Thousand million ton miles	%	Thousand million ton miles	%
Road	875	72	1,480	83	19.7	36	64	65
Rail	289	24	166	9	22.8	42	12.2	12.5
Coastal shipping	41	43	58	3	12.9	22	16.2	16.5
BWB waterways*	10	1	5	–	0.2	–	0.1	–
Pipeline	2	–	84	5	0.1	–	6.3	6
All modes	1,217	100	1,793	100	54.7	100	98.8	100

Source: Report of the Inquiry into Lorries, People and the Environment, HMSO, 1980
* Excludes waterborne freight traffic on tidal navigations and major estuaries inland of port limits

Table 1.6   Numbers of lorries and goods vehicles (thousands) – by unladen weight

	1960	1979
Lorries		
Up to 1½ tons	757	1,153
1½ to 5 tons	534	309
5 to 8 tons	41	114
Over 8 tons	11	121
All goods vehicles	1,342	1,697

Source: Report of the Inquiry into Lorries, People and the Environment, HMSO, 1980

vehicles (from 15 per cent in 1960 to 8 per cent in 1979), their size and weight has given them an impact which is one of the greatest perceived environmental transport problems today.

The effects of the change in transport use and mode are reflected in employment. The numbers at work in both road passenger transport and the railways have declined. The railway labour force has declined from 240,000 in 1971 to 206,000 in 1980 and is planned to be further reduced. Road passenger transport also employs fewer people and so does road haulage. Only in air transport (which includes those employed in the air services from Britain to other countries) has there been an increase in the workforce over the last ten years. Private cars, now so important in the total transport picture, require no employees to drive them, although their servicing is reflected in the larger numbers employed in the 'miscellaneous'

Table 1.7   Employment in transport (thousands)

	1971	1980
Railways	240	205.9
Road passenger transport	236	208.6
Road haulage	253	214.2
Sea transport	89 }	141.5
Port and inland water	97 }	
Air	75	88.5
Miscellaneous	119	186.4
All transport	1,110	1,045.1

Source: Transport Statistics 1970–80

category of transport employment (see Table 1.7). Overall, transport as an employment source has declined to 4 per cent of the total employed in all industries and services.

The changes of the last thirty years have shaped ideas, caused concerns, raised problems and led to new demands on the public services and on politicians at both national and local level for their solution. In the 1950s and 1960s, the focus was on the increased benefits brought about by the spread of car ownership. The motoring organizations and their allies in the car and construction industries picked up their pre-1939 campaigns for greater expenditure on road maintenance and improvement and on new roads. Traffic management to relieve congestion and improve the flow of vehicles and more parking facilities were also prominent in the campaigns of the time. The roadbuilding programme which commenced in the 1950s promised 4,000 miles of motorways by the 1980s. But soon other views began to emerge. While the politicians were preoccupied with housing and redevelopment as the main local issues, the public started to register their concern with other aspects of the deterioration of their environment. In Sheffield, for example, a 1968 survey of electors identified roads and traffic as the most important local issue and the one likely to be the most important in the near future, while local councillors placed it only fifth in importance, well behind housing, education, rents and redevelopment (Hampton 1970). A 1972 national survey found that road traffic came top of the list of factors which people most disliked about their environment (surpassing even unpleasant neighbours!) and poor transport facilities followed closely behind (Dept. of Environment 1975). These concerns soon focused on specific problems. The issues which emerged have come very much from the grass roots and through the activities of local pressure groups and voluntary associations of many kinds. Often they have clashed with the received wisdom and accepted view of both politicians, professional advisers and government officials, causing conflict and sometimes near-violent confrontation. The sectional interests of the motor vehicle, construction, airlines and road haulage industries have at times been ranged with government officials against local residents' groups, with the politicians in the middle, at first supporting the official proposals but later shifting their ground as the vehemence of public pressure became known. The history of motorway and airport proposals during this period very much reflects this pattern of conflict. Often the conflicts have resulted from a misreading of public views. For example, because car ownership is popular and traffic congestion disliked, it was assumed that there would be indefinite support for roadbuilding. The big plans for a motorway network launched in the 1960s and the Buchanan proposals for urban roadbuilding of 1963 were based on this premise and governments of both political complexions and numerous local authorities planned accordingly. That particular impetus was slowed down and often reversed in the 1970s as the opposition built up. Sometimes it was a case of a national policy clashing with very local interests, as in the third London Airport proposals which were fought with such passion by the local defence groups.

In the case of road proposals, the machinery for consultation and objection proved inadequate as a means of expression of protest. In repeated episodes at road inquiries at Epping Forest (the M 16), the Aire valley, Winchester (the M 3), Chichester and the Archway Road, residents' groups demanded the right to discuss the need for the roads and not just their proposed line. Police were called on more than one occasion to eject objectors. Events escalated in an unparalleled fashion for such hitherto sedate inquiries. At the Archway Road inquiry in 1977, the inspector first refused to allow new evidence on the need for a new road to be presented, and the resulting disturbance was so continuous that he retreated from the public hall to a smaller room with the public excluded to continue hearing objections from official bodies. Even in his aptly-named 'bunker' he was not secure: some objectors forced their way in and the inspector retreated further via a fire escape to a private room where he locked himself in. Two objectors (one a certain Councillor K. Livingstone) alleged that they were punched by an enraged Department of Transport official and brought charges of assault in the Magistrates' Court. (These were later withdrawn after discussion.) The inspector's reappearance in the 'bunker' next day was guarded by three lines of policemen and commissionaires. Meanwhile the objectors in the public hall who were allowed to listen to the inquiry proceedings through a public address system, brought to the occasion – in default of the discussion they were denied – a near festive, if desperate, mood. It was reported that 'objectors who had been enlivening proceedings in the main hall with puppet shows, sale of food in aid of their legal fund and angry shouts, struck up on a piano and a Renaissance rebec. Objectors danced, showering a confetti of torn-up paper (which they later cleared up)'[1] After several days the inspector withdrew his earlier ruling on new evidence and adjourned the inquiry for four weeks. He was never to come back to it. All these astonishing events took place in sober, middle-class Highgate. The participants, often to their own surprise, found a militancy far removed from their quiet professional lives and hitherto associated by them with the wilder kind of political activists: these middle-class residents were, in short, unknowingly radicalized.

A more recent issue, the question of subsidies to public transport services, has been quite as tumultuous. The lead has been taken by Labour-controlled local councils attempting to redress the balance of disadvantage of those of their constituents without cars, and to secure viable public transport systems by substantially increasing the subsidies to them. The clash has taken place between a government determined to secure cuts in public expenditure, aided by its political allies among the local councils and ratepayers' groups, and a series of equally determined councils able (as they thought) to provide the subsidies from locally determined tax revenues. The legal challenge to local powers eventually decided by the highest court of the land has gone against the local authorities and caused infinite confusion and uncertainty in the town halls. The supremacy of Parliament ensures that it will only be resolved in favour of the councils if a new statute can be enacted which fully authorizes the subsidies. Although the struggle has been a more conventional one between political party views and different levels of government, it nevertheless again highlights the new importance of a transport issue in terms of powers and public expenditure.

Nor have the earlier struggles of the environmental and residents' groups been convincingly won. The third London airport remains very much on the books. Stansted, the original choice of 1963, is now again the choice of government and a public inquiry is once more being held in 1981/83. No one knows whether the resistance of local residents will be mounted as vehemently for the second time and, if so, whether it will succeed. Although the road-building programme has been wound down largely because of the pressure to cut public expenditure, it could revive with national economic recovery and under the impetus of such projects as the Channel tunnel. The controversy over the government's efforts to increase maximum permitted lorry routes continues to produce strenuous concerted opposition. Continuing losses by British Rail and the financial difficulties experienced by both nationalized and privately-owned airlines keep the transport operators in the news headlines at national level.

The picture is still one of change and tumult, and there is little reason to think that it will end. The oil shortage, further changes in industrial structure, the impact of the new telecommunications all suggest that more radical changes are on the way which will inevitably be reflected in political issues and conflicts. By the end of the twentieth century we may come to recognize the controversies as a part of the social and political dynamic of our time.

NOTES

1. *Hampstead & Highgate Express*, 27 May 1977.

Chapter two

GOVERNMENT TRANSPORT POLICIES

The idea of a national policy for transport is a relatively new one. It recognizes the importance of travel and communication in twentieth-century society and acknowledges the interrelation and complexity of the various modes. It reflects the impact of the new transport systems on the processing, assembly and movement of goods, on living patterns and on residential communities. It accepts the significance of the transport industry to the national economy in terms of its capital investment needs, contribution to costs, numbers employed and as an area for fiscal product and regulation by government.

Government regulation of different aspects of transport has existed for many centuries past. The repair of roads, for example, was the subject of the Highways Act of 1555 which required land-owners to contribute their wagons and horses and all others to contribute their labour annually for that purpose. From 1835 the parishes were given the duty of levying a rate and hiring a surveyor and labour for road maintenance. Turnpike trusts, financed by private capital, which built the highways of the eighteenth century and charged a toll for their use, were regulated by Acts of Parliament. Canal navigation and railway line construction were similarly the subject of statutory authorization. The regulation of railway activity was a function of central government from 1840 onwards when a Railway Department was established within the Board of Trade to establish and enforce safety regulations and lay down requirements which companies wishing to open new lines had to meet. Nor was the element of social provision neglected. Gladstone's Railways Act of 1844 gave the Board of Trade powers to make railway companies run one 'parliamentary' train on every weekday which would stop at every station and would levy a fare not exceeding one penny per mile. Railway rates and charges were regulated by a government judicial agency from 1873. When the first road vehicles appeared, an Act of Parliament was quickly passed in 1865 to limit the speed of the new 'light locomotives' to 4 mph and to require a man carrying a red flag to precede them. After the appearance of cars on the roads in the early twentieth century there was a long struggle to remove or raise the speed limits set by law. Very soon too, the question of how road surfaces suitable for the new vehicles were to be financed became a problem of urgency for local authorities which quickly found its way into government fiscal policy and the struggle over the road fund.

The need for a policy for all forms of transport has developed from the accelerated impact of the new transport forms on all patterns of economic and social life. If there were no government policies, competition between rail, road and air transport could over a period determine which survived for long-distance, commuter, tourist, freight or other transport purposes. But such competition has often been destructive of the environment, has led to the duplication of services and been wasteful of resources. Moreover government could not pretend to a neutral position. Its policies on taxation, on the regulation of charges, on the statutory framework within which the transport undertakings had to operate and lately on grants to local authorities were, and are, crucial to the determination of transport systems and their survival. Government has therefore had to accept its role as central to the transport scene and to seek to devise policies which will express and further the national interest. The question, as always, is to decide what the objectives of national policy should be and how they should best be furthered.

The first attempt to devise a national programme and plan for transport was made at the end of the First World War when Lloyd George appointed Sir Eric Geddes to head a new Ministry of Transport in 1919. Geddes had his sights on a 'positive' transport policy, one which would promote the new motorized transport form and encourage the most efficient combination of rail and road use. The original scheme, which had Lloyd George's backing, was to nationalize the railways and canals and to bring roads, harbours, docks, shipping and civil aviation within the new department's regulation. It did not survive in the newly elected House of Commons of 1918 and the very limited measure which emerged as the Ministry of Transport Act was without either the public ownership of the railways or government powers to co-ordinate the various transport charges. But Geddes did succeed in bringing within one department both road and railway regulation. At the time, the combination of the two was seen as a defeat for the roads interest. The Road Board set up in 1910 had hoped for an independent role as a builder of new and improved roads financed by the proceeds of car and petrol taxes directly assigned through the road fund for the purpose. Motorists' organizations feared that the new department would mean the end of the impetus to road improvement through the use of hypothecated revenues. (They were right – the first 'raid' on the road fund was made in 1926 by Winston Churchill's Budget.) But twenty-five more years and another world war were to pass before the measures envisaged by Lloyd George were again put forward.

The idea of a national transport policy was not, however, lost during the inter-war period. Herbert Morrison, who was Minister of Transport in the minority Labour government of 1929–31 and Leader of the LCC from 1934–40, was its strong proponent. Morrison had seen the effects of the competition and conflict provided by 195 bus undertakings and the tramways and railways in London in the 1920s. His policy set out in a ministerial speech to the House of Commons on 12 December 1929 set out three principles.

1. Uneconomic and unnecessary competition must be eliminated.
2. The objects in view could be best achieved by securing unification under public control of passenger transport by omnibus, tramway or local railway in the Local Traffic Area. A single and simple form of public ownership should therefore be substituted for the complicated network of separate private and municipal interests now existing.
3. The principle of public ownership should be combined with the principle of commercial management, thus ensuring the advantages of vigorous business enterprise.

And more broadly for the nation he envisaged that (Morrison 1933: 88–9)

> A unified comprehensive transport system would concern itself primarily not with capturing traffic for this or that form of transport, but with determining the most economical and efficient method of meeting this or that public requirement. . . . Our conclusions about the organisation of transport nationally must be in the direction of a single ownership for the purpose of securing co-ordination, unification and managerial freedom which are essential to success.

Morrison was to achieve his aims for London in the London Passenger Transport Act, 1933 which established a monopoly of public transport in the London area for the new London Passenger Transport Board's buses, tramways and light railways acquired from the private companies which had operated them (but which excluded the main-line railway companies). The Act, largely prepared during his period as minister, laid responsibility on the board for providing 'an adequate and properly co-ordinated system of passenger transport for the London Passenger Transport Area'.

The London situation provided valuable experience of combining and co-ordinating separate enterprises into one passenger transport undertaking under public ownership. During 1939–45 the Coalition government operated a different co-ordination by taking powers to issue policy directives to the railways which were operated by a Railway Executive Committee, and by requisitioning and directing the use of long-distance lorries.

By 1945 the Labour Party was ready to implement its election manifesto programme to bring into public ownership all inland transport operations – rail, road, air and canal – and to co-ordinate their activities, while the Conservative Party could only confess that they still had to work out the detailed plans for a system in which every kind of operation 'would play its appropriate part'.

When the new Labour government came to formulate its Transport Act, 1947, the ideas of Morrison, the architect of so many of Labour's nationalization schemes, were firmly set out in it. The 1947 Act established a British Transport Commission with the clear aim (echoing the 1933 Act) of providing 'an efficient, adequate, economical and properly integrated system of public inland transport and port facilities within Great Britain'. The railways, docks and canals were nationalized and placed with all their subsidiaries in the ownership of the commission, but with separate executive boards to run them. Road haulage was partially nationalized: the long-distance lorries were operated as a public monopoly by British Road Services (BRS) within the structure; public and contract carriers operated by private enterprise were licensed and restricted to operations within 25 miles of their bases, but firms which ran lorries solely to transport their own goods were left entirely free of restrictions. The aim of road haulage regulation was to prevent open competition between road and rail over the long-distance hauls and to regulate it over the shorter distances. The exclusion of 'own account' hauliers (the 'C'-licence holders who transported their own goods) from any restriction was not originally intended, but the opposition of the Co-operative Societies combined with the Road Haulage Association (RHA) to secure their release from the 40 miles restriction proposed in the Bill. More than twice as many privately operated vehicles were thus released from any controls compared with the numbers subject to it and were free to compete with BRS lorries and the rail freight services. (The device of limiting and licensing private enterprise competition was also used for air transport services. The Civil Aviation Act, 1946 allowed private companies to operate under licence for charter and other work provided they did not compete with British European Airways' (BEA's) domestic scheduled services.)

In two respects, the Act was weakened by concessions made against Morrison's wishes while he was away ill. One was the exclusion of 'own account' hauliers and the other was the failure to give the British Transport Commission (BTC) substantial powers in relation to the services run by the separate executive boards. It took more than a statement of intent for integration of the services to overcome the ingrained professional values of life-long railway-men, docks and road haulage experts. Both these concessions laid the ground for the subsequent denationalization of road haulage and the further break-up of the BTC by Conservative governments.

Since the 1947 Act, the development of government policy has centred round five major themes. First there has been, as in so many aspects of British public life, a continuing preoccupation with, and controversy about, the proper role and size of the public sector in the transport industry. The Conservatives denationalized the profitable long-distance road haulage services in 1953 and removed BEA's monopoly of domestic scheduled services in 1960. The next Labour government (1964–70) introduced a further public sector role in 1968 for the purpose of road and rail freight integration in the form of the National Freight Corporation (NFC), and for bus operation through combining ninety-three bus undertakings into the National Bus Company. The 1968 Transport Act also established the Passenger Transport Authorities (PTAs) as a form of local public supervision and control of passenger transport services in urban local authority areas, and in 1969 authority over London Transport was transferred to the GLC. The advent of a very radical Conservative government in 1979 brought the prospect of partial 'privatization' of British Airways (BA) through the Civil Aviation Act, 1980 which changed the corporation to a public company and allowed a minority of the shares to be offered to the public. The subsidiary enterprises of British Rail such as Sealink, the Hovercraft and British Transport Hotels may now have a minority shareholding of private capital and the National Bus Company will be able to establish similar subsidiaries. The NFC has also been denationalized, but its employees have formed a consortium and have bought the company. These changes in government policy are the result of political changes in government and largely reflect Labour and Conservative doctrinal views on the merits of the public ownership of industry.

The second major theme, partly linked to the first, concerns the relative merits of competition and co-ordination in furthering the agreed aim of 'efficiency' in the operation of the transport systems. Labour governments have consistently sought to achieve efficiency, in Herbert Morrison's terms, by eliminating 'wasteful' competition and through the integration and co-ordination of the different branches of transport provision. Such a policy is clear in the brief given to the BTC in 1947, the role of integration of freight transport assigned to the NFC and the Freight Integration Council in 1968, and of integration of passenger transport services allotted to the local PTAs.

It is also to be seen in the emphasis placed by the TUC on coordination in 1965, when it recommended 'a newly constituted British Transport Commission' (TUC 1965). Although the TUC proposal was not taken up in the 1968 Transport Act, the Labour government picked it up in its proposal in the Transport Policy Consultation Document of 1976 to set up a National Transport Council as a 'high-level forum' representing all transport and user interests and, in more muted form in the 1977 transport policy White Paper, as a possible proposal for a transport 'little NEDDY' (a committee of the National Economic Development Office). A further resolution at the TUC in 1980 favoured an 'integrated' transport policy. In 1982, a joint TUC – Labour Party Report recommended the setting up of a National Transport Authority to advise the Secretary of State on investment needs and on the proposals of the transport industries in the light of government policy objectives. It should also monitor local transport services and advise on the provision of road haulage operator licences. The report recommended the new authority to include representatives of management, trade unions, local authority and user groups (TUC – Labour Party 1982).

The Conservatives on the other hand have distrusted co-ordination especially within monopoly provision, and have sought to increase competition in relation to publicly owned systems. The transfer of road haulage to the private sector in 1953 as a competitor to rail was one such measure, and allowing competition between public and private airlines on scheduled routes was another. In their 1955 election manifesto, Conservatives spoke of the 'spur of competition' to help stimulate efficient railway, roads and airways services. Some twenty years later, Norman Fowler, soon to become minister of transport, set out the conservative view that 'Efficiency is best secured by giving the user maximum choice and allowing maximum competition' (Fowler 1977). Accordingly, the 1980 Transport Act allowed the de-licensing of express bus routes and competition between local bus services.

Conservative governments have scrutinized the public enterprise transport concerns with a very sharp eye for financial viability and inefficient practices. The Beeching Report of 1963 *The Reshaping of British Railways* measured the railway operations in terms of their profitability. Since 1980 the Competition Act has introduced special powers for the Monopolies Commission to investigate inefficiency and the abuse of power in nationalized industries. The 1980 report on British Rail's South-East Commuter Services was the first to be carried out, followed by others on local bus operators. The Serpell Report on Railway Finances (1983) reverted to the Beeching approach.

Labour governments on the other hand have sought to scrutinize the private sector very carefully by introducing measures to check standards and practices. In 1968, for example, one condition for the licensing of heavy lorries was a record of adequate maintenance and the 1977 White Paper proposed further measures of control over both operators and vehicles. Accordingly, two independent committees of inquiry were set up, one on Road Haulage Operators' Licensing (The Foster Report 1979) and another on Lorries, People and the Environment (The Armitage Report 1980).

The third theme concerns the relationship between road traffic and roadbuilding and the environment. A most striking development in transport policy has been the sudden emergence of proposals for an extensive programme of roadbuilding in the 1950s and an almost equally fast onset of doubts in the 1970s about its impact on the environment. The Conservatives were the first to pick up the effects of the explosion in car ownership of the 1950s and spurred on by the advocacy of the BRF and the motoring organizations, put in their election programme for 1955 a promise to start 'the first big programme of road construction since the war'. Labour followed in 1959 with a criticism in their manifesto of the inadequacy of the government's roads programme and promised to relate roadbuilding to a national transport plan. In 1964 the Conservatives were pledged to treble the urban roadbuilding programme and to apply the principles of the Buchanan Report to town development, and both Conservatives and Labour in 1966 and 1970 continued to stress the need for an expanded road programme. Labour, however, continued to press as well in the 1960s for improved public transport services, especially for journeys to work.

In their enthusiasm for the Buchanan Report *Traffic in Towns* (1963) the politicians neglected what was perhaps its most important message. The report pointed out that the amount of traffic which could be accepted in towns was limited, and that more could only be accommodated if substantial physical changes were made, i.e. 'the canalisation of longer movements (of traffic) on to properly designed networks within which, by appropriate measures, environments for a civilised urban life can be developed' (Buchanan 1963: para. 443). But it went on to emphasize that 'the level of vehicular accessibility a town can have depends on its readiness to accept and pay for the physical changes required' (ibid: para. 444). The politicians picked up the proposal for urban roads and consequent town redevelopment, which accorded well with the current policies for rebuilding town centres and redeveloping housing, and forgot the report's warning that the scale of reconstruction could be 'somewhat frightening'.

Enthusiasm for new roadbuilding continued into the 1970s and it was not until the impact of the new roads was perceived in the towns that political party policies began to shift in varying degrees. The programme of orbital motorways for London, for example, was started by a Labour LCC in 1964 and continued by a Conservative GLC administration after 1967. It was only when the potential effects of the ringways were discovered and exposed through vigorous opposition by local groups that the Labour Party in Greater London switched its policy and ran its successful 1973 election campaign on a 'Stop the Motorways' platform. All round the country, the 1960s plans of local authorities of both political complexions to build new roads in towns on 'Buchanan' lines were arrested and turned round by the fierceness of public reaction. Not only traditional conservationist groups in historic towns such as York and Bath, but also a multitude of residents' groups responded at a very local level to the effects of the proposals on their living environment. The turning point for the national parties was the 1974 elections. The Labour Party's policy changed in the second 1974 election when it declared itself against the building of urban motorways. Its review of the level of expenditure on new roads was said to give priority to a network for heavy lorries. The Conservatives acknowledged the 'noise and nuisance' caused by new roads and promised to seek to diminish it by establishing lorry routes and other measures, but they also pledged the completion of a major road network.

Party policies at national level have had to cope uneasily with a conflict of popular wishes: on the one hand the desire of citizens as individuals to own and run cars, and to reap the economic benefits of lorry transport, and on the other their wish to be protected from the impact of traffic on their town centres, villages, residential and living areas. Labour governments have been more ready to adopt policies of restraint. Barbara Castle's period at the Department of Transport from 1965–68 was marked not only by an increase in restraints designed to increase safety, such as annual tests on cars over three years old and the introduction of 'breathalyser' tests to detect drunken drivers, but a requirement for local authorities to consider the needs of pedestrians and public transport users in drawing up their transport plans. The 1977 Labour government White Paper put as a major objective of policy the need to minimize the damage caused by transport to the environment, and proposed a series of measures 'for civilizing the heavy lorry'. Conservative governments have given support to the road haulage interests but have been increasingly aware of public reactions to large lorries. Their policies have therefore tried to protect the environment while not opposing the further expansion of road transport and road building. The 'Dykes' Act, 1973, for example, required local authorities to propose special routes for heavy goods vehicles to reduce their environmental impact. The Conservative government since 1979 has approved some increase in motorway construction but its consciousness of the environmental issue has also been apparent in the addition of eighteen new by-passes to the proposals, expected to benefit over 200 towns and villages. The by-passes must, however, be seen as part of its package of proposals in 1982 to raise the maximum permitted weight for five-axle lorries in Britain to 38 tonnes (Dept of Transport 1982).

The fourth theme which has emerged more explicitly than previously is the connection between transport policy and economic growth. Attempts to assess the direct economic benefits from new roads have been made by cost benefit analysis appraisals since the M1 Study of 1960 which measured the costs of reduced journey times. These appraisals do not, however, attempt to assess the effect of new roads on new economic development. But the connection between good transport facilities and economic growth is often held to be axiomatic and has been used to justify roadbuilding in the development areas as a way of attracting industry and employment. Grants from the EEC for regional development have been directed to improved communications on the same assumption. The economic decline of the inner cities and more generally throughout the country since the 1970s has brought this policy issue into greater prominence. It is interesting to note that the Transport Policy Consultation Document issued by the Labour government in 1976 does not mention economic development as an objective of transport policy but stresses social, environmental and resource objectives. But in the White Paper on transport policy a year later, the objective of economic growth and higher national prosperity has moved from nowhere into first place as one of three principal objectives, preceding the objectives of meeting social needs and preserving the environment. Perhaps this sudden pre-eminence marked the realization by the Labour government of the country's growing economic plight and its adoption of the Industrial Strategy. The new Secretary of State for Transport, Bill Rodgers, representing a constituency in the North-East of England, was convinced of the relevance of good transport infrastructure to economic development. Whether it is well based is open to question. The Leitch Report on Trunk Road Assessment (1977) was critical of the view that new roads foster growth and thought that the effects of roads on economic development should only be included in an assessment where there was strong evidence to justify it. The Conservative government's 1980 White Paper *Policy for Roads*, however, adhered to the view that new roads foster growth and described one purpose of its roadbuilding programme as 'to regenerate regions and bring jobs'.

A fifth policy theme which has recently become both urgent and vehement concerns the extent and nature of subsidy from public funds for passenger transport services. Conservative governments have regarded deficit financing and subsidy of British Rail, for example, as a sign of its failure and have urged it in all manner of ways, backed by cuts in subsidy and limits on its borrowing, to achieve commercial viability. Only subsidies for certain clearly defined types of social provision have been acceptable, for example, the pensioners' bus passes. Labour governments have been more accepting of general subsidies for social purposes. The 1968 Transport Act, although opposed to general deficit financing, opened the door to subsidy by authorizing grants to keep railway lines that were not viable in commercial terms open in cases where hardship might arise from their closure. It also gave the new PTAs powers to maintain unremunerative services and to subsidize them from the rates. The intention behind the subsidies policy was twofold: to keep passenger transport services available in the face of competition from private cars which had had a disastrous effect on their viability, and to provide for the transport needs of those without ready access to private motoring. The indirect effect hoped for was to keep public transport as a counter to the pressure of cars on roads, which was proving to be injurious to the environment. The 1974 Railways Act in the light of British Rail's continuing difficulties provided for a general subsidy to meet its deficit.

The Labour government's 1977 White Paper on Transport Policy affirmed its support for subsidies to public transport (except for inter-urban services) and to keep increases in fares at a low level. It proposed this support as 'a substantial and continuing commitment', though not an open-ended one, which it justified in terms of one of its principal objectives, namely 'to meet social needs by securing a reasonable level of personal mobility, in particular by maintaining public transport for the many people who do not have the effective choice of travelling by car' (Dept of Transport 1977: paras 14, 9). Local authorities in urban areas have used their powers to subsidize fares and for many Labour controlled authorities, such as South Yorkshire and the GLC, low fares have become an important part of their political and transport strategy. The Department of Transport (and the Treasury behind it) were, however, always concerned about the possibility of open-ended subsidies and pressed many local authorities in the period 1977–79 to limit and reduce their subsidy grants from the rates. The advent of the Conservative government of 1979 has sharply reversed the policy of subsidy and this has been one important strand in the conflict between Michael Heseltine as Secretary of State for the Environment and the urban, Labour controlled local authorities.

In 1981 the issue of subsidy came to a head when the newly elected Labour GLC put into action the Labour manifesto pledge to reduce London Transport's fares by 25 per cent by applying a subsidy. When the Department of the Environment cut back its block grant in an effort to prevent the move, the GLC proceeded defiantly to levy a supplementary rate precept of 6.1 p to meet the bill and maintain its electoral commitment, and the 'Fares Fair' reductions took place. Bromley Council then entered the contest with a High Court action designed to test the legal validity of the GLC's move by challenging its discretionary powers to levy the extra rate. When the GLC's action was sustained by Lord Justice

Dunn and Mr Justice Phillips in the High Court, Bromley Council went on to the Court of Appeal where Lord Denning referred to the duty that the GLC had to promote 'integrated, efficient and economic transport facilities' (section 1 of the Transport (London) Act, 1969) but which did not include 'the question of social or philanthropic or political objectives'.[1] The GLC had not held a fair balance as it should between conflicting interests. The fares cut 'was a gift to the travelling public at the expense of the general body of ratepayers'.[2] More significantly, as part of the court's judgment Lord Justice Oliver drew attention to the council's obligation to see that London Transport complied with its duty under section 7 of the Act to break even as far as possible. When the GLC went on to appeal to the House of Lords, Bromley's case was unanimously upheld. The Law Lords reinforced the view that, although the GLC had powers to make grants to London Transport, they should not be for the purpose of social or transport policy but to cover any unavoidable deficit. The 'fiduciary duty' of the council to balance the interest of its ratepayers and the beneficiaries of services was also emphasized. In the words of Lord Scarman[3] it is:

> a duty which requires it to see that the services of its instrument, the executive, are provided on business principles so as to ensure, so far as practicable, that no unavoidable loss falls on the ratepayers . . . for it is plain that the 25 per cent overall reduction was adopted not because any higher fare level was impracticable but as an object of social and transport policy. It was not a reluctant yielding to economic necessity but a policy preference. In so doing the GLC abandoned business principles. That was a breach of duty owed to the ratepayers and wrong in law.

For political drama, the GLC case could not be surpassed. Here was a left-wing Labour council seeking to put into action policies newly approved at an election and clashing with the 'undemocratic' Law Lords who had ruled in favour of another (Conservative) council's appeal with the enthusiastic approval of a Conservative government pledged to cut back public expenditure especially by local government. Here was a local council seeking to use its taxable resources, not for the humbler duties of repairing roads and emptying dustbins, but to put into practice the important transport policy of low fares which would help to keep the system viable, reduce traffic congestion and benefit Londoners without cars in direct opposition to a government aiming at the competition of market forces. On the sidelines stood the departments of central government dismayed about the levels of local government expenditure and far less enthusiastic about the transport deficits and cheap fares policy. But if high drama took place at the political level (and continued as the GLC launched its 'Keep Fares Fair' campaign in an effort to persuade Parliament to pass new enabling legislation, and numerous campaigning groups sprang into action), it would be difficult to overestimate the confusion into which the councils and their transport operators were plunged. If the GLC subsidies were illegal, what local council subsidies or indeed what local expenditure of any kind could be held to meet the criteria of 'fiduciary duty' and be legal? Other councils anxiously reviewed their policies and extended consultations took place with legal counsel; one authority was said to have received final legal approval of its annual budget by telex from a QC travelling abroad. In Merseyside, a similar legal challenge mounted by Great Universal Stores to the fares subsidy policy failed in the High Court largely because the 1968 Transport Act (as distinct from the 1969 Transport (London) Act under which the GLC operated) was differently phrased. While it required that the transport services should break even 'so far as practicable', it did not place on the metropolitan county councils the duty to secure 'economic' facilities, but 'to secure or promote the provision of a properly integrated and efficient system of public passenger transport to meet the needs of that area with due regard to the town planning and traffic and planning policies of the councils of constituent areas and to economy and safety of operation' (section 9 (3)). Nevertheless, doubts about the law caused several councils operating under the 1968 Act to consider raising their fares: West Midlands and Greater Manchester did so, but South Yorkshire decided against and do did Merseyside, after rejecting the advice of its leader who promptly resigned.

In London, differences of legal interpretation of the Lords' judgment were reported between the GLC and London Transport: was any subsidy at all to be deemed as within the law? The Secretary of State for Transport, David Howell, appealed to for legislation to clarify the issue, would only agree to introduce a Bill to make concessionary fares for pensioners legal and to allow for a large loan to be raised, repayable over five years, to meet the cost of repaying the £125 m. debt now deemed to have been incurred by London Transport. In so deciding, the government was trying to cope with its own political dilemma; if it was clearly seen to be responsible for the proposed 100 per cent rise in London Transport fares and for the loss of pensioners' bus and tube passes, it would lose in popularity among London Transport travellers what it had gained among London ratepayers. A series of smaller, less dramatic rises in fare and rate levels and the preservation of the pensioners' position was clearly preferable. The GLC accepted the legal authorization for the pensioners (now enacted) but, partly to emphasize its political position and partly because of an impassioned plea against borrowing for revenue purposes from its comptroller of financial services, turned down the loan and adhered to its 100 per cent fares rise. But although the leading chief officers of the GLC and the chairman of London Transport took the unprecedented step of issuing their own statement supporting the council's need for amending legislation, the London Transport chairman had doubts about the continued control of its affairs by the GLC. He proposed the transfer of the control of London Transport to the Department of Transport, and a Transport Policy Board including local authority representatives to be appointed by the secretary of state to buy in public transport services from London Transport, British Rail and the National Bus Company with both local authority and national funds. It would decide on service and fare levels (House of Commons 1982a). His ideas were developed further when the House of Commons Transport Committee later proposed a Metropolitan Transport Authority which would, among other functions, take over control of London Transport from the GLC. (House of Commons 1982b).

By the spring of 1982, tension had reduced. The fare rises took place with token protest and sullen compliance. An uneasy lull lay over the future of subsidies to urban transport until the autumn. Then the issue revived as the GLC, following consideration of a medium-term transport plan and consultation procedures, announced new plans to reduce fares in 1983 with the backing of fresh legal opinion as to its legality. Almost simultaneously, the government introduced a new Transport Bill to set 'guidelines' for revenue grant subsidies by all local transport authorities. The stage was thus set for a further clash between two diametrically opposed views.

If we compare the objectives set out for the British Transport Commission in 1947 – 'to provide an efficient, adequate, economical and properly integrated system of public inland transport and facilities' with the pre-occupation with social and environmental goals and with transport subsidies in the transport policies of the 1970s and 1980s, the differences are immense. In Herbert Morrison's world, the transport system was seen as relatively finite. It was assumed that a government body had the competence to order and organize an efficient and co-ordinated system provided all the pieces could be assembled within the control of that authority. It was assumed that the demand for transport services would be relatively stable. The effects of growth in road transport on the environment and on living patterns were not anticipated, nor was its effect on land use. The task was perceived as a limited one, to bring order and harmony into a series of competing, overlapping and conflicting services and to run them efficiently.

Thirty-five years later, government policy has had to extend its vision to a vastly more complex pictures. The effects of car ownership and the switch of freight to road transport have radically changed the viability of the earlier transport systems, and has raised the question of the very survival of existing towns and cities. Politicians have had to seek to answer certain very basic questions. Was the rising expectation of car ownership infinite and could and should it be met? How far and by what methods could cars and lorries be restrained? Could governments afford to let the public transport systems decline and die? What is the basic need for mobility and at what cost could increased mobility be achieved? How much public expenditure should be devoted to transport? How much of its energy resources could the nation allow to be spent on transport? Was the public and its elected representatives prepared to see and live with radical changes in the structure of cities and in rural communities resulting from transport changes, and what was it prepared to do to prevent, restrain or redirect them?

With all these new preoccupations, governments were still not able to say that they had solved the earlier problems which the 1947 Act had set out to meet. The 1976 Transport Consultation Document pointed out that 'we still appear to lack a proper framework for the co-ordination of transport policy both at national and local level'. The problems, it appeared, were not only becoming more complex but had not been successfully dealt with even in the simpler terms in which they were posed thirty years before. It is not therefore surprising that the pursuit of successful transport policies has been an arduous and controversial quest over recent years.

NOTES

1. The *Weekly Law Reports*, 15 January 1982, p. 68
2. Ibid. p. 70
3. Ibid. p. 123

Chapter three

TRANSPORT SYSTEMS AND THE GOVERNMENTAL FRAMEWORK

The planning, finance, operation and regulation of transport has come to involve a growing number of statutory authorities in a variety of ways. Before 1945 the chief function of government was to regulate the operations of trains, buses and airlines largely run by private firms. The greater involvement of government in transport matters has developed for several reasons. First, the programmes of nationalization set up a series of State-owned public corporations to act as transport operators. Government authorities have therefore become directly involved in the financing of the transport undertakings, in their prices, policies and investment programmes and in the regulation of competition between the public and private sector enterprises. Second, government's growing concern with both economic and land use planning has furthered a close interest in transport planning. Decisions on regional planning, road networks and the siting of airports have become the close concern of both central and local government. Local authorities in particular have in the last twenty years found that transport has jumped from an engineer's item at the bottom of their agendas to highly political and controversial issues at the very top. Third, the accession of Britain to the EEC has added a further dimension of policy through the consideration and implementation of EEC proposals for harmonization.

THE TRANSPORT OPERATORS

The railways

The Labour government which came to power in 1945 was committed to nationalization of the railways. The Transport Act, (1947) transferred all railways and their subsidiary assets such as shipping and hotels to the ownership of a new public corporation, the British Transport Commission (BTC). The operation of the railways was entrusted to a Railways Executive. The new management had the task of amalgamating the four railway companies and of standardizing their often very different equipment and practices. It had to face the problems posed by an extensive, often underutilized, Victorian railway network challenged by the competition from road transport, and to plan for a programme of investment which would not only replace and standardize its equipment but also modernize it after the wear and tear of the war years, and which would look to the railway transport forms of the future.

In terms of traffic carried, the railways have sustained their position reasonably well in total passenger transport mileage (see Table 1.1 p. 5) with a relatively small drop in the total mileage carried. They have lost out heavily in the competition for new traffic, with a drop in the share of the greatly increased market from 18 per cent in 1954 to 7 per cent in 1980. The most profitable passenger transport services now carried by British Rail are the inter-city services between main urban centres. The commuter service remains in deficit because of the demands placed on equipment for a very limited peak period operation. Freight services have shown an absolute decline with a drop of nearly half both in tonnage carried and in ton-miles, and the share of the market held by rail freight in ton-miles has dropped very dramatically since 1953 from 42 to 12.5 per cent (see Table 1.5, p. 11).

During the 1950s, the railways investment programme grew only slowly and was, in retrospect, inadequate to provide the new and modern equipment that was required. Moreover, increases in charges that would have kept the operating deficit under control were subject to the delays caused by their required consideration by the Transport Tribunal, a quasi-judicial body established under the 1947 Act to scrutinize proposed rate increases. By 1961, although road passenger transport mileage was virtually the same as in 1948 when nationalization took effect and freight tonnage carried was down only slightly, the financial situation had deteriorated to an overall deficit of £135 m. An investigation was started into the financial profitability of different parts of the railway service. The famous Beeching Report *The Reshaping of British Railways* appeared in 1963. In the same year, Dr Beeching was made head of the new British Railways Board which was set up following the dismemberment of the BTC under the Transport Act, of 1962. The 1962 Act did confer several benefits on the railways. It helped the

Board with its substantial debt burden through a financial reorganization which wrote off £475 m. The Board was also allowed to manufacture goods to meet its own requirements, and to operate its services on a commercial profit-seeking basis.

The Beeching Report made a dramatic impact on a public accustomed to an extensive but underutilized network. Its examination showed a heavy concentration of use and profitability on a relatively small section of the existing network. It found that one-third of the route mileage carried only 1 per cent of total passenger mileage; on over half of the mileage the fares and charges collected did not cover the fixed track and signalling costs and the costs of over half the stations were greater than the receipts they generated. Of the different types of business, the stopping passenger trains and general-merchandise freight traffic were highly unprofitable. On the other hand there were profitable aspects, namely the express trains between main centres of population, the carriage of coal and bulk goods and of whole train loads of goods assembled at private sidings. Beeching's analysis aimed (British Railways Board 1963)

> to shape the railways to meet present day requirements by enabling them to provide as much of the total transport of the country as they can provide well. To this end, proposals are directed towards developing to the full those parts of the system which can be made to meet traffic requirements more efficiently and satisfactorily than any available alternative form of transport, and towards eliminating only those services which, by their very nature, railways are ill-suited to provide.

The report referred to the possibility of running the railways for 'total social benefit' in order to prevent the greater costs of road congestion and roadbuilding, but it applied this concept only to the unprofitable commuter services and not to the social costs which might follow the closure of, for example, branch lines in rural areas.

The Beeching Report was accompanied by a set of radical proposals. Over 5,000 of some 21,000 route miles should be closed to passenger traffic and 2,363 out of 7,000 stations. Traffic would be concentrated on the best-used routes in order to minimize the high costs of the fixed-route systems, and on through-routes in order to minimize the high costs of stations and depots. Much of this programme was carried out by 1967, 72 per cent of stations specified for closure had closed and 84 per cent of passenger services identified were withdrawn. Under Dr Beeching's regime a limited network of maximum use was substituted for the all-embracing comprehensive railway system inherited from the nineteenth century. As a result, staff numbers were reduced from 477,000 to 269,000 between 1963 and 1969. But still the goal of profitability eluded the Board. Except for 1969 and 1970, the railways went steadily deeper into the red.

Beeching's commercial approach to the railways stimulated many local opposition groups. The 'Save our Services' campaign mounted by the National Council on Inland Transport was aimed against rail closures and gained the support of 150 local authorities (Kimber, Richardson and Brookes 1974). It coincided in time with the emerging opposition to the new motorways, and a realization of the environmental effects of traffic congestion caused by the increasing numbers of cars and large lorries on the roads. The 1968 Transport Act was designed both to assist British Rail and to ameliorate the environmental and social problems resulting from the switch to road transport which were now increasingly apparent. First, it empowered the government of the day to make 'social service grants' to the railways to keep open unremunerative lines whose closure would cause hardship provided these services were separately specified in the accounts. Second, it gave a similar power to the new Passenger Transport Authorities (PTAs), which were to be set up in the conurbations, to meet the costs of uneconomic but socially necessary rail services from local authority rates with the possibility that they would be reimbursed from central government funds. Third, it established a new public enterprise, the National Freight Corporation (NFC), which was designed to work together with the Railways Board to further the 1947 ideal of an integrated system of road and rail freight transport. The Board was also encouraged to a commercial marketing approach by a Prices and Incomes Board report of 1968 whose recommendations led to more selective pricing policies.

The approach to subsidy was further developed in the Railways Act, 1974. Under a new system of 'public service obligation' (PSO), grants could be made for unremunerative passenger services, to provide a service comparable to that in 1974. However, there has been subsequent criticism of the way the grants have been applied. The Select Committee on Nationalised Industries commented in its Report of 1976–77 that they had been directed to the passenger services as a whole and that insufficient consideration had been given to the needs of particular areas and the minimum service levels required. British Rail has noted that the 'net cost' payment of PSO over the whole system has the effect of spreading investment too thinly (British Rail 1981a).

Subsidies to the railways from government rose rapidly from £75 m. in 1970 to over £400 m. in 1975. In some despair, the government Consultation Document on Transport Policy of 1976 noted that the subsidies for 1976–77 would take about two-thirds of all the subsidies available for inland surface transport, for a system which carried only 8 per cent of passengers and 18 per cent of freight movement. Both the subsidy and railway investment were pegged at the 1975 level in real terms. Financial targets were set for the Board and it was encouraged to concentrate its attention on its most profitable sectors, such as inter-city passenger services, and those which it was best fitted to handle, such as commuter services and bulk freight, and to maximize revenue by increasing fares and selective fare reductions at off-peak periods. The 1977 White Paper on transport policy confirmed the continuation of a high level of revenue support and promised no major cuts in the rail network.

Since Sir Peter Parker became chairman of British Rail, his period of office has been marked by strenuous attempts to live within the financial limits, combined with pleas for higher investment, particularly for an extensive electrification programme. By 1979 the PSO subsidy had been kept to some £400 m., but it rose further from 1980–82. Productivity was claimed to have improved: manpower was down to 207,000 in 1979 and a further reduction of 38,000 was planned over five years. Flexible rostering of train drivers' duties was secured in 1982 after a bitter dispute with ASLEF. British Rail pressed for an increased investment programme between 1981–90. Its main campaign for electrification was supported by a joint report of British Rail and the Department of Transport in 1981 which took the view that 'a substantial [electrification] programme would be financially worthwhile' for 80 per cent of passenger and 70 per cent of freight services. The government in 1981 agreed to a start on the programme in East Anglia. Other projects which British Rail wanted to see in operation were a single-borerail Channel Tunnel (which is likely to be financed by private capital), the advanced passenger train (APT), more freight system modernization, a North–South London rail link and air traveller 'gateway' services to Gatwick and possibly Stansted.

The board is also pressing for a new definition of the PSO which would set targets for performance and standards of service for the more profitable services. For the unprofitable 'social railway', it wants a contract which would make payments linked to maximum passenger mileage, but weighted according to different types of traffic carried, such as rural services, commuter and leisure journeys (British Rail 1981a). A redefinition of the 1974 directive is also urged by both the Monopolies Commission and Serpell reports.

British Rail did not escape the privatization impetus of the 1979 Conservative government. Its subsidiary activities, such as Sea Link, British Rail Hovercraft, British Transport Hotels and British Rail Property Board were turned into companies owned by a British Rail holding company which could at British Rail's decision invite subscription private capital. The NFC was turned into a private company. The south-east commuter services were scrutinized by the Monopolies Commission and were reported in 1980 to be in need of tougher quality control and better staff management, more stringent pricing and more net revenue efficiency. The Serpell Report (1983) made suggestions for improved efficiency and cost reductions. It argued, as did the Beeching Report in 1963, that a cut in government grant would necessitate a substantial cut-back in the rail network.

Road public passenger transport
Bus and coach services have suffered from the competition of private motor cars even more than the railways since the 1950s. Passenger mileage has declined both in absolute terms and more sharply as a proportion of the total passenger transport picture (see Table 1.1. p. 5). Buses today compete for road space in the cities with taxis, lorries and cars on congested roads. Long-distance coach services compete for the most heavily trafficked routes while the rural areas suffer diminishing services. Car pooling arrangements, minibuses owned by some private organizations and contract coaches hired by others replace the regular stage bus services of former years in the smaller towns and the countryside.

The 1968 Transport Act attempted to stabilize the position of the bus services by providing for a stronger operating unit and framework. First, the National Bus Company was set up in 1969 as an amalgamation of a large number of local stage bus services, many previously owned by local authorities. By 1980 it owned 15,600 buses and coaches operating in 35 regional companies. Second, the 1968 Act provided for the setting up of PTAs in the large conurbations which were to plan and co-ordinate the passenger transport services in their areas. Third, government financial grants for new buses were made for a limited period to enable bus plant to be renewed and, in particular, for the change to one-man operation to be made. The hope was that a combination of rationalization in routes and management, economies through one-man operation and some subsidies to fares would enable the services to remain viable and provide at least a basic network of routes. The reality was that one-man operation, adopted in some eight out of ten National Bus Company buses by 1980, provided fewer savings in cost than was expected. Although the number of employees was reduced, higher wages had to be paid to one-man operators for the extra responsibility. The loss in bus speed, caused by longer waits at bus stops for loading, increased the cost in mileage terms. The estimated expected savings of 30 per cent have had to be revised to a lower level of 10–14 per cent and are at their lowest in the big cities where traffic congestion is greatest and the loading time is most expensive (Gwilliam and Mackie 1975). Subsidies to keep fares low have been extensively adopted by the metropolitan local authorities, varying from a projected 2p to 16p per passenger in 1981–1982, but have more recently come under fierce attack from the government and challenge through the law courts (see Ch. 6).

While subsidies have led to increased use of the buses, other factors are also important such as good service levels and reserved trafic lanes in congested streets. The problems of the rural buses have been greater, with rapidly diminishing levels of service. There has been little planning of services according to objective criteria of need by the county councils, low levels of subsidy compared with the metropolitan counties, and little co-ordination between the National Bus Company and other bus services, or between bus and rail (Rigby 1980).

A useful national reappraisal of bus services has come from the National Bus Company's market analysis project which has used data of passenger use, basic social data and attitude surveys to identify need and to re-plan its networks. The company has also used its analysis data to discuss with the local authorities which service times as well as which networks they wish to support financially. This kind of analysis of services and approach to subsidy is likely to prove the right approach for the future.

Following the 1980 Transport Act, the licensing system for buses has been loosened to allow for more competition and there has been a big increase in cut-price long-distance coach services. The 1982 Transport Bill proposes to give the National Bus Company power to set up new companies with the participation of private capital. It is expected that this will be used to introduce private capital into National Express, the company's long-distance coach service which has been competing successfully in the new market with a 25 per cent increase in passengers carried.

Road haulage

The growth of the road haulage industry and the dramatic shift in freight transport from rail to road since 1945 has posed problems both for the industry and for successive governments.

Road transport hauliers were first brought under licensing and control by the Road and Rail Traffic Act, 1933 in order to control vehicle standards, the wages and conditions of service of employees, and to regulate competition within the industry and with the railways. Under the 1947 Transport Act long-distance haulage by public carrier lorries was brought into public ownership. Lorry fleets of some 40,000 lorries were run as British Road Services (BRS) by the Road Haulage Executive of the BTC. For the rest, private sector operators who were public or contract hauliers or who used lorries partly for their own business and partly for public hire were limited to hauls of 25 miles from their base. A group of traders owning twice as many lorries again were allowed to operate lorries without mileage restrictions to carry their own goods only.

However, the Conservative Party was pledged to denationalization and, following the Transport Act, 1953, a Road Haulage Disposal Board sold off units of up to 50 lorries each to private ownership, although BRS was allowed to retain some 10,000 vehicles. The 1953 Act removed all restrictions on mileage for private hauliers and in 1968 the previous licensing system was replaced by a system of stringent 'quality' licensing for all vehicles of 30 cwt and over, which was aimed at securing higher safety standards.

The 1968 Act also made renewed attempts to protect the freight traffic of the railways and to 'co-ordinate' road and rail freight transport by three measures. It set up the NFC to act as a holding company for some fifty road and road–rail haulage public enterprises such as National Carriers, Roadline UK, BRS, Pickfords, Tartan Arrow and Freightliners. The object was to establish joint road–rail freight operations based on the growing container trade. The NFC was jointly charged with the Railways Board with securing or providing 'properly integrated services' for road and rail haulage. The NFC has a mixed record. Its early profitability declined after 1972 and it was reconstructed in 1978 when the Freightliner interest was returned to British Rail. Its performance then improved, but in 1980 it was denationalized, and its employees successfully bid for its ownership. It remains an umbrella organization for a number of haulage interests, with a turnover two or three times as great as any private haulage operator. The other measures introduced in 1968 were largely abortive. The Act introduced a system of 'quantity' licensing for all vehicles of 16 tons and over which was subsequently dropped by the Conservative government of 1970. It also set up a Freight Integration Council to advise on the provision of integrated freight services in the public sector, including the NFC, the railways, docks and waterways, air services and The Post Office. This council met only twice. Attempts to achieve the Morrisonian aim of 'co-ordination' have thus not succeeded.

The road haulage industry is largely run by professional hauliers who are predominantly small operators. Professional hauliers held 46,000 out of 138,000 current licences in 1977 but they moved some two-thirds of all goods carried and over three-quarters of goods carried more than 150 miles (Price Commission 1978). Of the professional hauliers, 55 per cent owned only one vehicle, 33 per cent between two and five vehicles and only 12 per cent more than six vehicles. The very large number of single-vehicle, driver-owned operators is one of the problems of the trade. Entry with a second-hand vehicle is easy but the vehicles are often poorly maintained, and regulations on loads, speeds and the number of hours driven are frequently not observed.

From the industry's viewpoint, public resistance to larger lorries is also a problem because they have a potentially higher productivity than smaller vehicles. The larger loads which the big lorries can carry is matched against the fact that labour, fuel and maintenance costs are little greater for large than for small lorries. The number of very large lorries over 8 tons has increased more than tenfold from 11,000 in 1960 to 121,000 in 1979 (see Table 1.6, p. 12). The industry's persistent campaign for an increase in the permissible size and weight of lorries has been met with fierce opposition from environmental groups and has had only limited success. The Armitage Report *Lorries, People and the Environment* (Dept of Transport 1980) made a number of recommendations for the improved design of heavy goods vehicles which would control their height, width, noise level, vibration and fume emission, and loading of vehicles and the speed limits at which they should travel. These recommendations were intended to pave the way for an increase in the permitted gross weight of lorries up to 44 tonnes for a 6-axle combination, 40 tonnes for 5 axles and 34 tonnes for 4 axles. The limit in the UK in 1982 was 32.5 tonnes, the lowest in any EEC country. Proposals for harmonization by the EEC have varied between a maximum 40 and 44 tonnes. The White Paper on transport policy of 1977 had refused to accept any increase in current limits but in 1982 new government regulations were introduced in Britain for an increase to 38 tonnes for 5 axles and 32.5 tonnes for 4, with the 6-axle weight proposal omitted.

The safety aspect of heavy lorries has given increasing cause for concern, especially the standard of maintenance, the regulation of lorry drivers'working hours and observation by the operators of safety regulations. In 1970 the EEC had enacted a directive requiring member states to put into force regulations requiring the installation and use of tachographs in all lorries and long-distance buses. (Tachographs are measuring devices which monitor the speed at which vehicles travel and the length and duration of the journeys made. They provide a check on the driver's observation of EEC regulations to keep within 8 hours driving in any 24-hour period.) The tachograph was vehemently opposed by both the transport workers' union and many road haulage firms in the UK and successive governments dragged their heels in implementing the EEC directive even after it was made compulsory in 1978, until the government was taken to the European Court of Justice.

Concern about the reliability of many haulage operators, particularly the small 'cowboy' firms, prompted an examination of road haulage operators' licences by a committee of inquiry. Its report in 1979 (the Foster Report) proposed more checks to vehicles, including roadside spot checks, and measures to penalize both firms and their employees in instances where the regulations were not observed. The government in 1980 adopted a number of recommendations in the Foster Report concerning roadside checks and vehicle identification and promised further study of the proposals on enforcement.

Although the Labour government's 1976 Transport Consultation Document affirmed that 'it remains the Government's intention that there should be an extension of public ownership in road [haulage] transport' no steps were taken to this end. The White Paper on transport policy (Dept of Trade 1977) spoke of removing subsidies to the movement of freight, whether direct or indirect, and recommended an increased vehicle licence duty related to lorry weight and the number of lorry axles which would secure a contribution from the trade sufficient to cover the cost of repairing damage to roads from lorries. It was hoped that this measure might help to put competition between road and rail on a fairer basis. The principle of increasing vehicle excise duty for each weight of lorry to cover its road track costs was also recommended by the Armitage Report of 1980 *Lorries, People and the Environment*, and was implemented in the Transport Act, 1981.

The road haulage industry has come to dominate the freight scene since 1945 with the exception of certain specialized cargoes for which rail can still compete effectively. Its problems have centred round the regulation of a large number of one-man operators, and the public's unwillingness to accept the very large lorries which the trade claims are more economical to its operations, or the new roads on which they most suitably run. It remains a thriving but unloved industry whose disadvantages are all too readily perceived.

Civil aviation

Civil aviation within Britain before 1939 was a tentative and insecurely based operation. A large number of small private airlines started and foundered against the competition between themselves and from the railways. Uncertain aircraft design and the lack of local airports were both hindrances to development. British Airways was a private company formed in 1935 which preferred to develop European rather than internal services. In 1945, consciousness of the vital part aircraft had played during the war led to a considerable degree of unanimity about the need to foster the air services of the future. The Civil Aviation Act, 1946 established British European Airways (BEA) as a public corporation (although the Conservatives would have liked to have seen it supported by both State and private investment) with a near monopoly of air transport within Britain and an obligation to equip the new airline with British-built planes. Private airlines were not initially allowed to compete with BEA's scheduled services but could be licensed by the newly established Air Transport Advisory Council to offer charter services. From 1949 the council was directed by the government to license companies to provide 'associated arrangements' on BEA routes provided they did not undercut the corporation's fares and rates. The private airlines tended to concentrate on charter and car ferry services and by 1959 flew about a quarter of total air passenger mileage. The Civil Aviation (Licensing) Act, 1960 continued the process of opening up civil aviation to competition by ending the monopoly of BEA on scheduled air services. Although BEA held its proportion of traffic on domestic air routes, its share of total passenger mileage fell because the private airlines expanded and consolidated in the growing charter service field. Competition to BEA was further encouraged by a government directive made under the 1971 Civil Aviation Act, provided the new Civil Aviation Authority (CAA) was assured that more than one service could be profitable. However, the next Labour government's directive warned the CAA of the desirability of avoiding unprofitable 'duplication'.

The 1980 Civil Aviation Act has abolished the government's power to make directives but has placed on the CAA certain statutory duties, including furthering the interests of air-traffic users, and publishing its policies on licensing. The benefits of competition are once again stressed. More importantly, the Act abolishes the public corporation status of British Airways (BA) and places it under the Companies Act, with a proportion of its shares open to public subscription. Since BA was in the red up to 1983, there have as yet been no offers.

In the twenty years between 1960–80, air passenger mileage increased from 8 m. passenger km to 28 m. a more than four-fold increase which exceeded even the dramatic expansion of private car mileage (see Table 1.1, p. 5). The reason lies in the usefulness of air transport for longer-distance journeys. In 1974, of 3.5 m. air passenger journeys on domestic air services within Great Britain nearly a half were between London and Scotland. Overall, routes based on London took 75 per cent of the total and connecting flights to London provided between a third of all the domestic traffic into London (Transport Policy, 1976). Although domestic air traffic is an expanding area, much of BA's domestic network is not profitable. In 1980, twenty-eight domestic routes ceased to operate. The services to the Scottish Highlands and Islands require subsidy and the government granted £4 m. to their airports in 1981–82.

Inland Waterway Traffic

The use of inland waterways for the transport of freight in Britain is minute compared with the substantial proportion of waterborne freight to the total in other European countries. After the great canal period of the late eighteenth and early nineteenth centuries when some 4,000 miles of canals were built, they have fallen steadily into decline. Today, twenty-eight of the navigable waterways are designated for pleasure cruising and recreation and only eleven are designated primarily for freight traffic; in 1979 some 5 m. tonnes were carried, over half of which comprised coal, coke, fuel and bulk liquids. This total does not include the much larger tonnage carried on tidal navigations and major river estuaries, either wholly within port limits or as part of a coastal shipping passage or from foreign ports. An estimate of the total freight carried on all such inland waterways in 1974 was 3,570 m. tonne km of which only 390 m. was on landlocked canals (Inland Waterways Association 1980). With the introduction of modern ocean tug-barge systems of container ships carrying barges, as well as seagoing barges, there is scope for the development of through-freight traffic from sea to inland sites without transhipment. The first major investment in canal improvement since 1905 was recently approved for the Sheffield and South Yorkshire Canal, with a 30 per cent EEC grant.

THE REGULATORY AUTHORITIES

The regulation of transport operators in the public interest is a function which pre-dates state ownership, but continues in relation to both publicly and privately owned operators. The need to ensure standards of safety has always made state regulation a necessary part of transport provision since the early days of the Railway Commissioners. The type of public organization used for this purpose is semi-autonomous, appointed by government but not directly answerable to it, and exercising quasi-judicial functions. Licensing, both for quality and quantity of service, co-ordination of services, the hearing of complaints and some executive functions are typical functions of these bodies.

Traffic Commissioners

The Traffic Commissioners were first established by the 1930 Road Traffic Act to license bus services. They have powers to grant, refuse, revoke and renew bus and all public service vehicle licences, to attach conditions to them and to license drivers and conductors. Standards of safety are foremost in considering 'quality'. 'Quantity' licensing for bus services aims to prevent duplication of services. Up to 1980 fares charged have been regulated by the commissioners. Since the 1980 Transport Act, the licensing system has been considerably relaxed in the interest of stimulating competition and new services. Express and excursion coach services no longer need a licence except for safety, and the commissioners are obliged to grant all new applications for licences unless they are judged contrary to the public interest. The fares charged by bus stage services need no longer be approved.

The work of the Traffic Commissioners is carried out in area organizations by representatives drawn from panels of local government councillors nominated by their councils, and with an independent chairman appointed by central government. The panels consider applications for licences for new services and for renewals for a variety of purposes. For example, the Northern Traffic Area in 1979–80 granted new licences for 111 new bus services, including 37 urban stage services, 33 related to bingo halls, 12 for workers' services, 13 for schoolchildren, 10 for excursions, 5 for long-distance express services and 2 related to greyhound stadiums, plus 26 new minibus permits for schools, universities, youth clubs, and voluntary services, 3 permits for post buses and 1 community bus service to link to a stage bus service (Traffic Commissioners 1980).

Civil Aviation Authority

The CAA was set up in 1971 as the successor to the Air Transport Advisory Council to regulate airlines and control safety in civil flying. It licenses new airline services and the 1980 Civil Aviation Act requires the authority to publish its policies on licensing and to set out the criteria on which applications are decided, having due regard to the benefits of competition. The authority has a statutory duty to further the interests of air transport users.

The police

Police involvement with transport derives from their role in the supervision of road traffic and from the need to enforce the law relating to traffic offences, especially in relation to speeding and parking. The proportion of police time spent on traffic work is considerable: a survey carried out in 1965–66 showed that it accounted for 23 per cent of time in the provincial police forces and 19 per cent in the Metropolitan Police district, compared with 28 and 31 per cent respectively for the time spent on work directly connected with crime, and 40 per cent in both cases spent on maintaining civil order (Martin and Wilson 1969). Since 1960, traffic wardens have been recruited to help control car parking and since 1965 they have also been allowed to direct traffic; in both respects they have been able to relieve the police of some part of their traffic duties. In 1981 there were over 4,000 traffic wardens in England and Wales.

The extent to which laws are enforced depends on the number of police available and the relative importance attached to the function at any time. In a study carried out in the USA in 1964, important differences in the policies of different police departments towards the enforcement of traffic laws was noted. The mean 'ticketing rates' (fixed penalty notices) for every 1,000 motor vehicles varied greatly from a rate of 36 in Massachusetts for groups of towns with a population exceeding 25,000 to 287 in Florida (Gardiner 1969). The variation was attributed to the resources allocated to traffic work, which reflected the importance attached to it, and whether there were specialized traffic police (who were more 'productive' in issuing tickets for offences). The American study noted the ambiguity of public attitudes towards the enforcement of traffic laws in comparison with laws relating to property or violence. The same is likely to be true in Britain. The report of the Royal Commission on the Police (1962) noted that the law relating to parking was not widely supported and its purpose was not accepted, and suggested that the wide degree of discretion left to the police was not satisfactory. The move towards an extension of the fixed penalty system for traffic offences (Dept of Transport and Home Office 1981) will save police time and cost but will not necessarily improve the uniformity of law enforcement in this area. Illegal car parking is now a considerable problem in London and it has been suggested that the effectiveness of traffic enforcement action by the Metropolitan Police should be monitored (House of Commons 1982b)).

Traffic schemes like road planning are the responsibility of local authorities. While the police must be consulted by them whenever new traffic schemes are proposed, their views are not necessarily followed. Police concern with the flow of motor traffic on the one hand and the prevention of accidents on the other has tended to advocacy of traffic/pedestrian segregation. The idea of pedestrian precincts separated from through traffic, for example, was emphasized by the Assistant Metropolitan Police Commissioner for Police in the 1940s (Tripp 1942).

STATUTORY CONSUMER REPRESENTATION

Attempts to see that consumer interests are heard in relation to the nationalized transport undertakings have been made from the time that the BTC was first set up. The 1947 Act provided for the appointment by the minister of a Central Transport Consultative Committee and one regional Transport Users' Consultative Committee (TUCC) for each of eleven regions which were required to consider and make representations to the minister on matters concerning nationalized transport organizations. The original remit of the committees allowed them to consider changes in charges and proposed reductions in services before they occurred but these powers were removed by the 1962 Transport Act, as was the right to consider road transport matters. Since that time, the committees have been restricted to a consideration of railway services but even here their competence is very limited. They may consider complaints about rail services and make representations to British Rail on them and on many aspects of service which affect the consumer, such as train punctuality and cancellations, catering services and provision for disabled travellers. But they have no powers to obtain redress for grievances or to see that their recommendations are enforced. In 1978, for example, the TUCC for the south-western area promoted the idea of a pre-addressed card to be made available at stations so that passengers could immediately submit complaints after a difficult journey. British Rail agreed to a three-month experiment but blandly reported at the end of the period that 'the benefit to management (and ultimately to the customer) of the information obtained from the cards was limited and did not justify the additional costs involved'. The experiment was brought to an end and replaced by 'an arrangement, to be conducted by the Board, aimed at increasing public awareness of the present arrangements for registering a complaint or comment' (Central Transport Consultative Committee 1979). A year later, it was reported by the board that

> the results of the experiment had not confirmed the need for additional advertising of the already established channels for the passenger who wished to complain or comment. The number of complaints received during this period had not contributed any information to management which was not already known. As a result, the Board were not proposing to extend the experimental procedure. (CTCC 1980).

The role of the committees is this circumscribed by their very limited powers, and by their remoteness from the travelling public. It says something for the persistence of disgruntled customers that the Committees were notified of 65,516 complaints received by British Rail in 1979 and 58,373 in 1980.

The CTCC has in recent years taken more positive initiatives in relation to its role by setting up sub-committees to consider specific topics. The idea of consumer performance indicators was put forward in 1979 as a way of measuring how satisfactory the services were, and it was suggested that British Rail should set and publish targets for each indicator. This idea was taken up and in 1981 Brit-

The politics of transport

ish Rail listed eight performance standards towards which they were working on commuter services (British Rail 1981). But in this, as in other initiatives, the TUCC is totally dependent on the goodwill of British Rail and the co-operation of the Department of Transport.

In the 1970s, several proposals to extend consumer organizations' influence over transport services were made. The National Consumers' Council (NCC), a statutory and government-funded organization set up to further the interest of consumers, proposed a consumer approach to transport (National Consumers' Council 1977). The first step should be the measurement of how far different transport modes met consumer needs. Then minimum national standards should be established for passenger transport provision and services provided to implement them. The NCC proposed the setting up of a National Transport Council to consist of the operators, the consumers and the government which would agree the standards to be achieved. It also wanted to see priority for public transport, improved provision for pedestrians and cyclists, and the replacement of several different taxes on motor vehicles by one tax on petrol.

The NCC and the CTCC both wanted to see bus services included in the TUCCs' remit, together with the power to consider fare changes and service cuts in rail services, and the right to be consulted by local authorities and PTAs (Select Committee on Nationalised Industries 1976–77). In 1978 government proposals were put forward in a White Paper to transform the CTCC into a National Transport Consumers' Council, able to consider and make recommendations on the tariff structure of rail services and on the services and facilities of bus and other operators. It proposed to empower county councils to set up advisory committees on their transport plans and the services in their areas, which would include both councillors and representatives of consumer interests and would liaise with the regional TUCCs (The Nationalised Industries 1978). These proposals did not give the consumer bodies all they wanted, but they were an advance on existing practice. However, they fell with the Labour government in 1979.

The present limited remit of the statutory consumer bodies therefore remains. For bus services, the Office of Fair Trading advises dissatisfied customers to contact the Local Traffic Commissioners, or, in London, the London Transport Passengers' Committee. Air travellers may have recourse to the Air Transport Users' Committee and the Airport Consultative Committees. Like the

48

TUCCs these bodies are outside the mainstream of political life and it requires a well informed and persistent citizen to make representations to them. Consumer representative organizations have fallen out of favour since 1979. 'Let the market decide' has been the maxim, and the Conservative government has devoted its policy to promoting competition to British Rail where possible, as with the decision to allow long-distance express bus services, and to the more abrasive examination by the Monopolies and Mergers Commission of the London and South-East Commuter Service. The apparatus of consumer representation, however, remains and the committees continue to make their representations and their muted comments to the beleaguered operators' boards and to the Ministers of Transport and Trade. As a point of pressure on government, they lack any powers and as a political pressure group they lack the representative quality and the immediacy of the informed citizens' groups on specific issues.

ROADS AND AIRPORTS

Roads and motorways

The road system inherited in 1945 was very much the same as that of before the First World War. New roads were increased by only 10 per cent mileage between 1911 and 1959. The main purpose of road expenditure was to improve the surface of roads and to make them suitable for cars and lorries and for much heavier traffic loads.

Once the effects of the boom in car ownership and use had become apparent, attention was drawn to increased road congestion and the need to remedy it. The first reaction was to improve the flow of traffic by 'traffic engineering'. The existing road capacity in towns was increased by a variety of measures such as one way streets, the phasing of traffic lights, and the building of traffic roundabouts, typically introduced by engineers in the local authorities. To increase the amount of road space available, the Road Traffic Act, 1954 empowered local authorities to introduce parking meters for short-term parking, the revenues of which would finance off-street long-term car parks for commuters. There was at this time no view that car commuters should not come into cities, only that they should be encouraged to park off the streets, thus keeping them free for traffic. Thus the Working Party on Car Parking in the Inner Area of London reporting in 1953 actually proposed only nominal charges for the commuter car parks in order to encourage motorists to park in them. Many local authorities made it a condition of planning consents for new office building that adequate car parking provision for employees should be provided. Expenditure on road 'improvements' was quite low at this time, well below the level immediately preceding 1939.

The next phase began when the authorities took the view that the existing road space, however well managed, would be insufficient for the projected traffic increase resulting from forecast levels of car ownership. As everyone was in favour of the spread of car ownership and use, the only feasible policy seemed to be to increase actual road capacity to accommodate it. In particular the idea of special trunk roads or motorways designed for fast through traffic came to the fore. The design for a motorway from London to Birmingham had been prepared by the Ministry of Transport back in 1938, based on the example of the German autobahns. Post-war plans for a ten-year programme of trunk roadbuilding which would form a 1,000 mile network had to be dropped in the austerity years. The BRF, in alliance with the motorists' organizations, began the pressure for a modernized road system which fell on fertile ground in the 1950s. New plans were made and in 1959 73 miles of the first motorway, the M 1 from North London to Birmingham, was opened to traffic. Motorway and dual carriageway roadbuilding proceeded with great impetus in the 1960s. In 1970 the then Labour government proposed a strategic road network of some 4,000 miles by the mid-1980s. Motorway mileage completed in Great Britain leapt from 95 miles in 1960 to 657 in 1970 and 1,543 in 1979, and dual carriageways increased from 1,720 in 1970 to 2,881 miles in 1979.

A further factor which encouraged the roadbuilding movement was *Traffic in Towns* (Buchanan 1963) which stressed the importance of separating through traffic from local traffic and the living areas of towns. Many local authorities interpreted this idea to mean that new or improved through roads were required which would draw off traffic from shopping and residential areas. Radial and ring roads appeared in large numbers of town development plans, often allied to proposals for redevelopment and pedestrian shopping centres. In 1960, for example, Nottingham Council approved a £68 m. plan for primary highways which included both radial and orbital routes, together with three links to the M 1 and four river crossings. The push to new road construction in towns to meet traffic projections reached its peak in 1969 with the publication of the Greater London Development Plan proposing new radial routes and three orbital ringways each with six- to eight-lane capacity. The gigantic cost and environmental effects of these grandiose plans provoked growing opposition to them and a successful struggle was waged against them (see Ch. 6). The abandonment of the London ringway plans by the GLC in 1973 also marked the effective end of the unlimited roadbuilding era. The new roads programme was scaled down in 1975. Public expenditure on trunk roads and motorways was steadily reduced in real terms from £635 m. in 1975–6 to £320 m. in 1980–81 (both figures at 1980 prices).

The change in national policy in the second half of the 1970s was paralleled at local government level. The big roadbuilding schemes were dropped and replaced by more modest ones, particularly in the cities. In Nottingham, for example, a new majority on the city council scrapped two large and expensive road schemes estimated to cost £190 m. at 1970 prices and produced in 1972 a policy document which proposed reliance on car restraint, traffic management and improved bus services with the city centre closed to through traffic (Grant 1977). The total expenditure on road construction and improvement by local authorities dropped from £540 m. in 1975–76 to £342 m. in 1979–80 (1980 survey prices) (HMSO 1980).

Since 1979, the Conservative government has reinstated the roadbuilding programme, but at a far more modest level: between 1979–80 and 1983–84, expenditure on motorways and trunk roads is projected to stay at some £400 m. per annum in real terms (HMSO 1980).

Airports

At the end of the Second World War, a legacy of numerous airfields built for military use were available for conversion to civil traffic to meet the tremendous boom in air traffic. In 1976 44 m. passengers arrived at British airports, 32 m. of them from international flights (Airports Policy 1978). By that date, there were forty-one major airports in the UK (including the Channel Islands), of which seven (including Heathrow) were owned and operated by the British Airports Authority (BAA) and accounted for three-quarters of all passengers, and twenty-three were operated by local authorities. By far the largest proportion of passengers came to London (31 m. or 70% of the total) and more specially to Heathrow (23 m. or 52%). After Heathrow, the most heavily used airports were, in order of importance, Gatwick (6 m.), Manchester (3 m.), then Luton, Glasgow, Jersey, Birmingham, Belfast and Edinburgh, each of which received over 1 m. passengers in 1977. The heavy concentration of air traffic on London and especially on Heathrow has caused problems since the 1950s. Successive governments have grappled with the difficult choices available to them. They remain unsusceptible to any generally accepted solution, or even resolution in the light of the many conflicts which parallel those experienced with the roadbuilding programme.

London's airport strategy in 1946 was to close the pre-war aerodromes of Hendon and Croydon and to convert the military airfield at Heathrow to civilian use. The decision to use Heathrow as a civil airport was first taken at a meeting of civil servants in 1943 which is reported to have lasted exactly 40 minutes (Jay 1980). By 1954, the need for a second London Airport led to the choice of Gatwick (Sussex) as a new one-runway airport. Ten years later, further traffic increases led a government interdepartmental committee considering a third airport to choose Stansted (Essex), an unsuccessful candidate for the second airport in 1953. Stansted was accepted by the government as the choice in 1967, but such was the opposition by the residents and their supporters in that rural area that the decision was taken to appoint a high-powered commission of inquiry which would use the very latest methods of evaluation to assess the problems and the options for different available sites.

The Roskill Commission appointed to enquire into the problems of a third London Airport reported in 1970 after exhaustive investigation in favour of Cublington in Buckinghamshire as the new airport site, but the government of the day preferred the minority report put forward by Colin Buchanan in favour of the coastal site of Foulness, largely on environmental grounds. In 1974 the next government overturned the decision for Foulness (now known as Maplin) as too costly and, in the light of revised estimates of air traffic and the introduction of larger aircraft with bigger carrying capacity, opted for a limited strategy of more efficeint traffic control and increased terminal capacity at existing airports. The 1978 White Paper on Airports Policy was the first national review of airport strategy. It rejected any new major airport for London and proposed a set of options for expanding existing airports: a fourth terminal for Heathrow, a second terminal for Gatwick, or more intensive use of existing airport facilities at Stansted and Luton. Further longer-term options would be a 'major expansion' at Stansted, conversion of a military airfield, or a 'new airport'.

In 1981, the government confirmed the fourth terminal at Heathrow but set limits to the further expansion of air traffic movements there. A second terminal at Gatwick was also confirmed, but no second runway. Stansted, the persistent choice of both the CAA and the BAA, was marked for limited expansion with a new terminal capable of handling up to 15 m. passengers per annum to be built in the late 1980s, but with a safeguarding of land for a second runway and for further terminals in the future. These proposals are again under consideration at a public inquiry and are likely to be as controversial as the earlier conflicts in 1967, 1971 and 1974.

London's airports have dominated the airports problem because of the weight of traffic coming into the London area. In the 1970s the possibility of diverting some of the traffic to airports in other British regions was urged. But the White Paper of 1978 found that 80 per cent of passengers ending their journeys in London had destinations in South-East England. In 1975, out of 29 m. passengers arriving in London, 13 m. were from overseas, of whom 10 m. came for tourist or non-business visits. The White Paper concluded that although the use of regional airports should be encouraged especially for charter and other tourist services, passengers with destinations in South-East England could not legitimately be diverted to airports outside the region. The continuing problem therefore remains the capacity and impact of London's airports, both present and future.

THE GOVERNMENTAL FRAMEWORK

All the transport operators are heavily circumscribed by law and dependent on government action. Law regulates their scope and powers, government decides the tax levels and allowances for petrol and motor vehicles, the investment levels of the statutory operators, and special grants and subsidies to them and takes decisions on the basic track and plant (e.g. roads and airports). The struggles between road and rail, motorized transport and the environment are focused on the vital policymaking decisions of government and are reflected in the changing structure of government departments and their relationships with local authorities.

Central government

From its establishment in 1919, when it took over both the regulation of the railways from the Board of Trade and the roadbuilding programme of the Roads Board, the Department of Transport has contained the rivalry between road and rail. In the 1960s and 1970s

53

the struggle between roadbuilders and environmentalists and the effort to reconcile their interests was reflected in the attempt to establish one large Department of the Environment in 1970 which was to include a broad span of functions including land use planning, the environment, oversight of the transport industries and the motorway building programme, as well as the housing and construction industries.

The new department had a secretary of state, three second-tier ministers, a staff of 73,000, over half of whom were professional and white collar workers, and disposed of 12 per cent of all public expenditure (Draper 1977). The transport duties were split between one minister who dealt with the nationalized transport undertakings, and another who included transport planning and road passenger transport in his local government responsibilities. Policy co-ordination was to be achieved by the secretary of state as presiding 'overlord', by a policy management group of officials whose job was to promote co-ordination by ensuring consultation between different policymaking groups, and by a strategic planning directorate which aimed to produce a Department of the Environment combined strategy by setting out the objectives of each section of the department and devising a common basis for the comparison of their inputs and outputs (Painter 1980a). At the political level the transport interest could be overruled by the secretary of state. For example, Peter Walker in 1970 overruled on environmental grounds the recommendation by the Minister for Transport Industries for higher permitted lorry weights.

But these arrangements to further integration did not succeed. The Highways Directorate, the only unit with executive functions in transport, kept its unit intact from the start and the transport function gradually withdrew from an integrated planning approach. By 1973 all transport functions were grouped back under one ministerial head. Within the department the transport side and specifically the roads programme suffered in the competition for resources because of the emphasis put on housing expenditure between 1973–76 by secretaries of state Rippon and Crosland. An earlier confidence in the unifying effect of large conglomerate departments had faded, and the replacement of Harold Wilson by Jim Callaghan as prime minister signalled a change of direction. The reversion to a separate Department of Transport in 1976 with a cabinet minister at its head made it possible for transport (and specifically the roads programme) to compete for resources at the political level on equal terms with other services.

The present situation leaves the approval of county structure plans (including long-term transport plans), housing, environment questions, the canals (considered as recreational provision) and local authority questions generally to the Department of the Environment. The Department of Transport has the responsibility for the overland transport industries – railways, freight transport, ports and passenger transport; for road planning and policy and the construction of motorways and trunk roads; for local and urban transport, including traffic management, parking control policy, lorry controls and transport grants to local authorities; and for road safety and the licensing of vehicles and drivers. The road construction work of the department is separately organized and housed. There is a chief highways engineer with a staff responsible for design, engineering standards, traffic engineering and control. The regional Road Construction Units (RCUs) set by in 1967 to prepare and manage major new trunk road schemes employed 2,450 staff in 1980, mostly engineers and other professional staff seconded from local authorities, plus 700 staff in 6 headquarters units and were responsible for the design and supervision of the construction of major new road schemes. In 1980 the government began to phase them out in favour of the use of private consultants and, in certain cases, county councils as agents. Although the motive was privatization, the effect could be to weaken the importance of road-building within the department by removing an important part of its executive responsibility for the programme.

Turning to the transport industries, the department exercises important powers in relation to British Rail. As a public corporation, British Rail's Board is appointed by the secretary of state and he has the power to issue policy directives to it. Financial control of British Rail's affairs is stringent because of its recurring deficit. The 1974 Railways Act, which requires British Rail to continue to provide a service comparable with that provided in 1974 and authorizes the government to pay a public service obligation grant to meet the net cost of doing so, also obliges British Rail to agree with the department criteria for framing and carrying out all proposals involving substantial capital expenditure. There are successive layers of cumulative control: the department sets the limit of the PSO grant, the annual ceiling for investment expenditure and a ceiling to the total of all external financing from sources outside British Rail's funds.

In relation to local authorities, the department effectively supervises their transport plans and expenditure through its approval of the annual TPPs submitted as a basis for the Transport Supplementary Grants (TSGs).

Two other government departments which have functions relating to transport are the Departments of Trade and Industry. The Secretary of State for Trade until recently had powers to give ministerial guidance to the CAA: these powers were abolished by the Civil Aviation Act, 1980 and replaced by statutory duties. As part of its responsibility for aviation, the department decides the policy on airports. British Airways also falls within its orbit as a public corporation (since 1980 potentially a private company with mixed public and private funding). The Department of Industry is also indirectly concerned through its responsibilities for the aircraft, motor vehicle, and engineering industries.

Finally, the Treasury has powers to control the levels of public expenditure, both revenue and capital, which are crucial to decisions on roadbuilding, rail investment, airport building, aircraft manufacturing, to the levels of transport subsidy, the level of petrol tax and of vehicle licence duties, and the tax reliefs afforded to the motorist.

The involvement of central government in transport matters is thus considerable. But, with the important exception of the building of motorways and trunk roads, it is not a direct responsibility for the provision of transport. The job of the departments concerned is to provide general policy outlines, to react to the plans of local authorities and transport operators rather than to initiate them, and to monitor the operation and effects of the services. A major problem has been to produce a national policy for transport which balances the conflicting objectives and integrates the different systems. For a short period from 1947–53, the newly created BTC might have taken on that role, since it was charged with securing an integrated transport system, but the BTC had to grapple with too many executive responsibilities and never looked like a policymaker. The removal of the bulk of road haulage operations to the private sector in 1953 effectively stopped the integration of the road and rail systems under one ownership and in 1962 the BTC was replaced by a series of executive authorities for the railways and other nationalized transport undertakings. National policymaking within the transport industries was represented for a period by a token and powerless National Transport Advisory Council (NTAC). The 1968 Transport Act came close to providing practical measures to co-ordinate road and rail and to sustain public passenger transport, and the 1976 Consultation Document on Transport, the policy review initiated within the new conglomerate Department of the Environment, made the attempt to set out national policy objectives. Partly at the instigation of the TUC, it also put forward a proposal for a new National Transport Council. Based on a National Economic Development Office type structure of management and trade unions, local government and consumers, with a minister as chairman, it was suggested that the council would scrutinize strategic proposals and problems, particularly relating to pricing and investment. A year later the proposal was turned down in the government White Paper (Dept of Transport 1977). Most recently, a TUC – Labour Party Report of 1982 recommended the setting up of a National Transport Authority. The recurrence of this type of proposal for co-ordination and a national policymaking body must be read as continued dissatisfaction with central government's policy guidance on transport matters and its inability to reconcile the claims on resources of the various operators and authorities, and to integrate the different transport systems into a national transport service. The failure during the period 1970–76 of the attempt to co-ordinate transport, planning and the other environmental services within one Department of the Environment signals the retreat from unified policy objectives in those areas. However, the impetus provided by the 1977 White Paper and the annual published roads programmes, plus regular scrutiny of the whole field by the new House of Commons Transport Committee, may together prompt the thinking on transport in strategic terms which has for so long been needed at national level.

Local authorities

Up to 1947, the only functions of local authorities in relation to transport were to build and maintain all except trunk roads and, for certain borough councils, to run municipal bus and tram services. The Town and Country Planning Acts now require the local planning authorities to include proposals for all kinds of transport in their structure plans, and to relate them to their policies for land use. Since 1972 the structure plans are the responsibility of the county councils. The counties are also responsible for the building and maintenance of all except some unclassified roads in their areas, although many district councils carry out road maintencance for the counties on an agency basis.

The 1968 Transport Act set up Passenger Transport Authorities for the conurbation areas and empowered them to promote and co-ordinate passenger transport services in their areas through Passenger Transport Executives (PTE) and (notwithstanding a legal challenge in 1982) to subsidize them. These authorities became the metropolitan county councils under the 1972 Local Government Act. The PTEs run bus services which may receive subsidy from the county councils. They may also assess the value of rail passenger services and may seek to reach agreement with British Rail and the county councils for financial assistance to support and develop individual services. In shire counties, the distribution of powers is different as there are no PTEs. The county councils have the responsibility of promoting adequate public transport services. They may subsidize the services and enter into agreements with the operators who are British Rail and the National Bus Company or other local bus operators. The situation in London is different again. Since 1963, the GLC has been the strategic planning authority, responsible for drawing up the development (now the structure) plan. The Transport (London) Act, of 1969 charged the GLC with the duty of developing policies to promote integrated, efficient and economic transport services and to produce transport plans. The GLC appoints the board members of the London Transport Executive and controls the general policies, budget and fares policy of London Transport. Until the House of Lords decision of 1982, it was thought that the GLC had full powers to subsidize London Transport's services. Although British Rail is required to notify the GLC of proposed changes in its fares or service levels, the GLC has no powers to enter into agreements with British Rail for the development of particular services although it may subsidize an existing service. The GLC is the highways authority for principal and metropolitan roads, as distinct from non-metropolitan roads which are the responsibility of the London boroughs, and is responsible for traffic management.

Since 1974 all county councils have been required to submit annual Transport Policies and Programmes (TPPs) to the Department of Transport for approval as a basis for the receipt of TSG, and since 1978 shire counties are required to produce Public Transport Plans (PTPs). The TPPs have proved to be a very useful exercise for the counties, requiring them to draw up corporate plans for transport in their areas which proceed from an identification of transport need and the problems arising from it to the determination of objectives and thence to proposals for the systems and services which will realize those objectives. The TPPs are intended as 'a series of interrelated proposals covering both capital and current expenditure over the whole transport field – public transport, roads, parking, traffic management, pedestrians' (Dept of Environment 1973) without a bias to any one kind of expenditure. They set out long-term strategies and five-year rolling plans for their implementation. The counties thus have the framework for consideration of an integrated transport policy.

One of the objects of the TPP system was to make the county councils think of all kinds of transport expenditure, not just of roadbuilding. Analysis of the planned TPP expenditure of local authorities between 1975–80 shows that the aim of eliminating 'bias' towards any one kind of expenditure on transport has been achieved. But intervention by the Department of Transport at an informal level in the way local authorities spent the grant as well as the amount they received was apparent even before the tighter controls inaugurated after 1980. For example, after 1975 the department was anxious to reduce the level of bus subsidies and it therefore considered them separately outside the expenditure guidelines, and refused to allow metropolitan counties to transfer resources from support for rail (which it favoured) to support for buses (which it did not) (Mackie 1980).

Within local authorities, the need to think out transport policy coherently in relation to planning and to financial resources combined with the powers of the 1968 Transport Act has had the effect of raising the importance of transport as a local authority concern. It has inevitably meant that decisions on the level of respective transport services have become more subject to changes in political control. For example, a switch from capital to revenue expenditure on highways and an increase in revenue expenditure on public transport occurred when Labour took control from the Conservatives on the GLC in 1973–77. When the Conservatives came back in 1977–81, the emphasis was changed back to capital expenditure on both highways and public transport (Wistrich 1978). In 1981, Labour parties in South Yorkshire, London and elsewhere put subsidies for public transport prominently into their local election manifestos and made them an issue of prime political significance, soon to be underlined by the legal challenges of 1981–82. The dramatic House of Lords decision on the GLC was enthusiastically received by a Conservative government strongly opposed to Labour transport authorities' policy on subsidy. The conflict between them was a clear example of the new importance of local authorities' decisions on transport matters which clashed with the government's aims in macro-economic policy as well as its political philosophy.

The politics of transport

The effect of UK membership of the EEC is that directives of the Community apply to national transport matters and that EEC grants are available to assist transport infrastructure projects in the UK.

Thè Treaty of Rome of 1957 which established the community stressed the need for a common transport policy which would remove obstacles to free competition between the community countries in the provision of transport services and would promote the development of the inland transport industries on a sound basis. Various 'harmonization' regulations have been introduced to assist the functioning of the transport market. For example, international road and rail goods tariffs have been harmonized, administrative formalities at customs posts have been reduced and a common European driving licence will come into operation in 1983 (European File 1981). A directive to limit and monitor lorry drivers' driving hours via the tachograph which was part of the harmonization of drivers' working conditions has caused particular problems in the UK. Because of the strenuous opposition of the Transport and General Workers' Union (TGWU), the government did not implement the directive until ordered to do so by the European Court in 1980. While the harmonization of safety standards for goods vehicles has been agreed, the problem of harmonizing permitted lorry weights and sizes remains a highly controversial one which has not yet been resolved. The EEC Commission's proposal of 1979 for an increase in permitted lorry weights up to a total of 44 tonnes has been backed by UK lorry manufacturers, but it would mean a substantial increase over the present permitted limit in the UK of 32.5 tonnes. As yet, agreement has not been reached by the Council of Ministers.

The EEC makes grants of two types to assist transport infrastructure projects. The first grants come from the RDF and are intended to improve transport facilities in regions of low prosperity in order to assist economic development. Several British areas have benefited from such grants, e.g. grants for roads and for harbour improvements in Yorkshire and the North-East. Another type of grant proposed but not yet realized is for transport projects of community interest which would improve international communications, eliminate bottlenecks and lead to energy savings. The latest proposal for a Channel Tunnel, which has already been evaluated by the Commission, might be one such project in the future.

Other EEC policies impinge on the transport sector. The Community's objectives for improving the environment have led to directives on the control of exhaust fumes from engines (1970) and of the sulphur content of gas oils (1975) (European Documentation 1977). Member states have been asked by the Community to study the environmental impact of all major transport infrastructure proposals before carrying them out. The objective of energy conservation is also recognized in EEC transport matters, although no Community action has so far been achieved to harmonize measures to save energy.

Thus the EEC is another political arena where decisions are taken which affect transport operators, their customers and those affected by their operations. To influence the policies of the Community, lobbies exist at European level both for the transport operators and for environmental groups (the European Environmental Bureau).

Chapter four
TRANSPORT PHILOSOPHIES

The problems posed by road transport traffic in the second half of the twentieth century relate to land use and living patterns, the structure and purpose of towns and the quality of the physical and social environment. Many different kinds of specialists and experts have made a contribution towards their solution, and their ideas have, quite naturally, been shaped by their own professional outlook. It is not surprising that civil engineers have seen the solutions in terms of roadbuilding, architects have put the visual qualities of townscapes first, and planners have related transport to land use. Bus and train operators have looked to the viability of their undertakings, the police have had to cope with traffic regulation and road accidents, ecologists have given priority to energy resources and naturalists to the conservation of flora and fauna. Philosophers have contemplated the condition of man in a motorized urban society. Politicians' views have reflected the pressures from interest groups, their own habitual clients and the broad trends of public opinion. The conflicts over the right policies to pursue have often resulted from the differing outlooks and ruling ideologies of the various groups. Some account of these is now given.

Transport philosophies have evolved around three central themes which are interconnected. The first is the view of the best living and working patterns that can be encouraged. The second is the shape of the physical environment, whether it is countryside or town, and the third and most crucial is the attitude towards road vehicles and, in particular, whether they should be welcomed, encouraged and allowed for, or whether their use should be restrained.

One of the first town planners of the twentieth century with revolutionary ideas about change in towns included important views on transport. Ebenezer Howard's *Garden Cities of Tomorrow* published in 1902, planned towns with a population of 30,000 with pedestrian access to work and to all facilities. Trams were to supplement walking within the towns, and roads and rail would serve the industry located on the periphery and would provide links to other towns. The first garden cities at Letchworth and Welwyn drew on these ideas. Taken across the Atlantic to the USA in the 1920s however, the concept made a vital adjustment to meet the needs of a population already adapting to car ownership. The scheme for Radburn, New Jersey, adopted in 1928, incorporated road access on a much larger scale with pedestrian and cycle networks carefully segregated, housing grouped in culs-de-sac, and full pedestrian facilities and access restricted to neighbourhood areas with populations of about 8,000. The Radburn layout, together with the idea of 'parkways' of free-flowing road traffic based on experience in New York and Chicago, then recrossed the Atlantic to become the basis of further thinking in Britain. The first generation of new towns after 1945 used a neighbourhood population of 5,000–10,000 as their basic unit, and many local authorities adopted similar schemes for new housing developments (Potter 1981). Some later new towns grouped their neighbourhoods into larger areas of 20,000–30,000 for pedestrian and cycle access, but Milton Keynes opened the town more fully to road access and car use through a grid of roads enclosing small centres of populations of only 2,000. The principles were, however, the same: residential and living areas and pedestrian ways were as far as possible to be segregated from road traffic which had its own designated routes. Parallel thinking also developed in relation to the traffic problems of existing towns and cities.

Decentralized garden cities or residential suburbs did not accord with some other ideas about city living. A very radical view was taken by the architect, Le Corbusier. In his outline for 'the city of tomorrow' first published in 1924, Le Corbusier envisaged a high-density city as both a business and residential centre protected by a green belt of woods and fields, outside which lay a series of garden cities on the periphery whose citizens largely worked in an outer industrial zone (Le Corbusier 1971). Corbusier was adamant that the new cities must be built on a geometrical layout with a grid-iron road system and a minimum of streets. Traffic would be classified into three types, each with its own kind of road: heavy goods traffic would run below ground; light goods, bus and car traffic would be at ground level; while fast traffic would be elevated on arterial one-way roads with accesses at about every 150 m from the ground. To complete the picture, there would be a railway station at the centre of the city with a flat roof for 'aero-taxis' linked to the main airport in the city's outside protected zone. Corbusier's vision was an architect's aesthetic of skyscrapers, surrounded by light and open space. His descriptions are usually from the air. Of his *Voisin* scheme for rebuilding part of the centre of Paris Corbusier wrote (1971: 280–1)

> Instead of a flattened-out and jumbled city such as the airplane reveals to us for the first time, terrifying in its confusion, our city rises vertical to the sky, open to light and air, clear radiant and sparkling. The soil, of whose surface 70 to 80 per cent has till now been encumbered by closely packed houses, is now built over to the extent of a mere 5 per cent. The remaining 95 per cent is devoted to the main speedways, car parks and open spaces. The avenues of trees are doubled and quadrupled, and the parks at the foot of the skyscrapers do, in fact, make the city itself one vast garden . . . Our city, which has crawled on the ground till now, suddenly rises to its feet in the most natural way. . . .

An immense transport system would supply the ideal city and allow its citizens easy access. And 'There need be no limit to the number of motor vehicles, for immense covered parking areas linked up by subterranean passages would collect together the host on wheels which camps in the city each day and is the result of rapid *individual* transit' (ibid: 187–8). Corbusier's visionary views were influential among architects for many years and inspired much post-war planning of towns with motorways and with high-rise housing, since fallen into disrepute.

The ideal of light and space, which Corbusier saw as requiring vertical form, was approached from a different angle by his contemporary, the eminent American architect Frank Lloyd Wright. Wright wanted space for living but spread horizontally and foresaw houses built at a density of one per acre: (1963: 127)

> imagine man-units so arranged and integrated that every citizen may choose any form of production, distribution, self-improvement, enjoyment, within a radius of, say, ten to forty minutes of his own home – all now available to him by means of private car or plane, helicopter, or some other form of fast public conveyance: . . . Such integrated distribution of living all related to ground – this composes the new city embracing this entire country: the Broadacre City of tomorrow

What both architects had in common was the concept of cars and roads as a liberating experience. In Wright's view (ibid: 147)

What nobler agent has culture or civilization than the great open road made beautiful and safe for continually flowing traffic, a harmonious part of a great whole life? Along these grand roads as through human veins and arteries throngs city life, always building, building, planning, working.

The encouragement of car ownership and the full use of cars was thus desirable and the building of highways to accommodate them a great enterprise of beauty and power. The expression of this philosophy is to be seen in the great intercontinental highways and the freeway systems of such American cities as Los Angeles.

Not all planners were carried away by the possibilities of speed, high-rise city life or decentralized suburban living. Lewis Mumford was critical of both these images (1968: 142)

One of them is the "City in a Parking Lot", a collection of highrise slabs and towers linked by multi-laned expressways; the other is the Anti-City, alias Megalopolis, a by-product of urban decomposition, which in the pursuit of nature denatures the countryside and mechanically scatters fragments of the city over the whole landscape.

But if the two visions, both of them exalting the highway and free use of cars was out, what was to replace it? An American writer, Jane Jacobs, has reacted by extolling the virtues of existing urban life with its intricate mingling of economic and social activities at street level (Jacobs 1964). Jacobs opposes the unrestricted access of cars and the segregation of pedestrians into traffic precincts. She has posed the two alternatives as either the erosion of cities through full car use and roadbuilding, more parking and less pedestrian space, or the attrition of cars through a system of planned congestion, aimed to reduce car traffic but not buses or essential lorries and to open more opportunities to pedestrians. Lewis Mumford on the other hand equally rejects this static philosophy and sees the solution in better-planned cities without freeways, with more pedestrian facilities and precincts segregated from traffic. He also favours garden cities grouped in networks along the lines advocated by Ebenezer Howard (Mumford 1968).

British experience broadly parallels American. In 1913, Sidney and Beatrice Webb asserted (Webb 1963: 254)

We cannot doubt that – whatever precautions may be imposed for the protection of foot-passengers, and whatever constitutional and financial readjustments may be necessary as between tramways, omnibuses, and the public revenues – the roads have once more got to be made to accommodate the traffic, not the traffic constrained to suit the roads.

The phase of enthusiasm for roadbuilding has, however, never reached the same heights as in the USA; car ownership has grown more slowly, there is less land and a stronger tradition of town planning to check the suburban sprawl of city building. Conservation of historic towns and of the countryside has figured prominently in British debates. The planner Thomas Sharp, for example, had the ideal of a high-density town culture to pose against the garden city. His purpose in a series of plans was to preserve the visual sense and physical character of the townscape, and he therefore proposed transport schemes which would divert road traffic from the key areas of old towns to new or existing designated roads. Sharp's espousal of the virtues of city life was based on a veneration of earlier cities (Stansfield 1981).

Mention has already been made of the Radburn layout and its concept of neighbourhood environment areas protected from traffic. A similar 'precinct principle' emerged in relation to city traffic organization in Britain. The author of this idea was H. Alker Tripp, the Assistant Commissioner of Metropolitan Police. Tripp's job was traffic regulation and his concern was with road accidents which he thought were caused by roads not built for modern traffic conditions. He saw the solution as planning a new system of roads and a traffic layout which avoided the need to impose legal restrictions and controls on vehicles. If roads were graded into a hierarchy of arterial, sub-arterial and local roads, and 'precincts' were established as safe havens for pedestrians between the arterial roads, the needs of traffic would be served and pedestrians would be protected. Tripp's arterial roads were designed for fast through-traffic without side street access, his sub-arterial roads were for slower traffic in the built-up areas and his approach or local roads were for slow traffic only which serviced the precincts. For the arterial roads Tripp foresaw '. . . the ultimate aim . . . is to make the vehicle tracks as well adapted, fenced and arranged for high speed, without danger to the general public, as the railways are; and at the same time to provide adequate road space for the vastly increased number of vehicles' (1942: 18). Within the hierarchy, pedestrians would be prohibited from the arterial roads, but their freedom would be greatly enhanced inside the precincts which would be free of through traffic. 'They will cease to be maelstroms of noise and confusion, and become companionable places, with an air of leisure and repose; such streets will provide a real promenade for the town dweller and a rest for jaded nerves. We shall be getting back to Merrie England' (ibid: 77). Tripp also urged that towns should have by-pass roads for through traffic, one on an outer circle and 'at least one good circular road . . . within the confines of the town itself, to enable the town's own traffic to by-pass the centre as much as possible' (ibid: 61). This by-pass should have 'full arterial status' and provide the terminals for radial roads into the city.

The problems of transport provision are seen at their most intractable in cities because of the many conflicts between the movement of road vehicles and the movement and living patterns of people. The opposing philosophies are to accept, accommodate and build for vehicle access, or to restrain and restrict vehicles in the interest of preserving the urban fabric and the free movement of individuals. But the compromises in between are many as people seek the benefits of cars without their disadvantages. The plans which have appeared have, to a greater or lesser extent, both adapted towns to traffic and restricted traffic in towns. At the centre of this process over the last twenty-five years has been Colin Buchanan, a civil engineer by training, with long experience as a public servant in planning, and later as a consultant and academic. Buchanan's ideas owed much to Alker Tripp, especially his principle of pedestrian and vehicular segregation.

The Buchanan Report *Traffic in Towns* came to the basic conclusion that

> the motor vehicle . . . is a beneficial invention with an assured future, largely on account of the great advantages it offers for door-to-door travel and transport. There is an enormous potential demand for its services, and we think a constructive approach to the problem of accommodating it in towns and cities is both required and justified (1963: 191).

Towns would need to undergo 'substantial physical changes' if they were to adapt to large numbers of vehicles, because existing arrangements were 'completely out of date'. The basic principle was that 'the level of vehicular accessibility a town can have depends on its readiness to accept and pay for the physical changes required'. The recommendations were firmly based on the building of new primary roads (albeit with 'aesthetic design'), in conjunction with 'the comprehensive development or redevelopment of large areas', and the restraint and restriction of much traffic to those roads so that the environment of the areas or precincts they surrounded could be protected and enhanced. Road hierarchies, pedestrian/vehicular segregation, traffic control and environmental management were the clear principles adopted, with flexibility on the amount of traffic restraint and new roadbuilding. The report received many plaudits. Its principles were advocated to local authorities by Ministry circular and many local schemes of the period were based on it. Wilfrid Burns, Newcastle's city planning officer, who later became the Department of the Environment's chief planner, praised it as 'a milestone in thinking, equal, in my view, to the milestone represented by Ebenezer Howard and the new towns movement' (Bruton 1981: 210) and adopted it as the basis for road planning in Newcastle. Buchanan as a consultant used it as a basis to plan for new roads in Bath and Edinburgh. But the use of Buchanan-type schemes went sour. One city council after another turned them down in the 1970s because they were unwilling to meet the financial and social costs of road construction and widening and the turmoil of redevelopment required, or the re-routing of traffic along hitherto quiet roads, and some completed schemes have been criticized as having an inhuman scale.

The new philosophy which emerged was closer to the American writer, Jane Jacobs, who rejected city redevelopment and new roads. Traffic restraint was put forward as the only acceptable policy, with the private car as the chief object of that restraint, and greater use of public transport was urged. Greater facilities and priorities for pedestrians and cyclists were advocated, both within traffic-free precincts and throughout the town.

Behind this movement was a very strong desire to conserve what was best and most familiar in the city environment, as well as a fear and distrust of new development. But there were other strands. E. J. Mishan, the economist, queried the price of economic growth. He thought that the external diseconomies of motor traffic and air travel far outweighed their benefits and reduced social welfare: '. . . the invention of the private automobile is one of the great disasters to have befallen the human race . . . The motor industry has come to dominate the economy as brazenly as its products dominate our physical environment and our psychology' (Mishan 1969: 222). Mishan draws a parable of the 'pistol society', where life revolves round the free purchase and use of pistols: society adapts to them, the economy depends on their production and 'pistol architecture' fashions the towns of the future. His parallel leads him to the view that

> The alternative of the Buchanan Plan emerging from this story is, quite plainly, not to seek to develop technological means of *accommodating* the mounting traffic, but, quite the contrary, to seek to contain it. Indeed, the one radical alternative we should take a long look at, before contemplating the range of compromise solutions that are feasible, is that

of a plan for the gradual abolition of all privately owned automobiles (ibid: 128).

Hostility to motorized transport is also shown by Ivan Illich, who speaks of the burdens of travel placed on the city commuter and the inequalities created by the possession and use of cars. In a society where the transport industry exercises a 'radical monopoly', it both creates and shapes the need it satisfies, and rearranges society for the benefit of those who possess transport facilities in large quantity (Illich 1974). It consumes vast quantities of energy supplies, clutters the environment with vehicles and roads and 'expropriates life-time at the behest of speed' (ibid: 80). Illich's answer is the bicycle, which is powered by its rider, labour intensive, thermodynamically efficient, equal in opportunity for all able-bodied people, and conducive to good social relations and participatory democracy. With bicycles people may 'become masters of their own movements without blocking those of their fellows' (ibid: 75). He does, however, allow for motorized free public transport especially for old people.

The energy issue also emerges strongly in the viewpoint of ecologists, who advocate restrictions on private transport, and the building up of public transport systems in order to conserve both materials and energy. The decentralization of cities and consequent reduction of the need for energy-intensive journeys is another part of the ecologists' outlook and policy (*Ecologist* 1972).

Although the Buchanan Report was widely interpreted as advocating new roadbuilding in towns, and policies based on such advocacy were subsequently frequently rejected, its real importance rests on its underlying assumptions and the problems it poses. The report accepts the maximum possible use of the motor vehicle, poses possible solutions to its movement in towns and asks what price the citizens are prepared to pay for greater or lesser freedom of car movement. That dilemma has still to be resolved, but the validity of the questions remain. Buchanan himself showed the limits that he was prepared to put on motorized transport in his opposition to the building of the third London Airport at Cublington, and later at Stansted. His view that 'it would be nothing less than an environmental disaster if the airport were to be built at any of the inland sites, but nowhere more serious than at Cublington' illustrated the importance he attached to conservation of the countryside and to land use planning (Roskill 1971: 154). He believed that the inland sites breached Abercrombie's policy of an outer country ring. Conservation of the nation's heritage became the overriding good: '. . . the land of the country, after its people, is its most precious asset, not to be squandered, not to be exploited, not to be sacrificed for short-term gains, but to be zealously guarded and enriched for passing on to succeeding generations' (ibid: 149). In his defence of Stansted in 1981 he moved on to query the importance of air transport itself (Buchanan 1980). Buchanan's conservation instincts applied to the countryside and were reflected in many of the battles against new motorways and airport building. Others concerned with the quality of life in towns have queried the basic assumption about maximum car use. They have pointed to the adverse effects of motor traffic, and the destruction of the physical fabric and environment of towns by roadbuilding. They have repudiated the Buchanan of *Traffic in Towns* and adopted the Buchanan of the London Airports struggle. The local residents' groups have formed up with allies along the spectrum of architects, conservationists, planners and many more in seeking support for their pleas against what they have seen as destructive change.

Dissident professional workers challenging the views of fellow specialists have helped to breach the wall of received opinion and reopen the grounds for discussion. In 1973, an Independent Commission on Transport was convened which drew on the skills and experience of people from many different professions. In their report, they challenged the concept of mobility, claiming that 'The real goal is not ease of movement, but access to people and facilities. Movement is desirable only to the extent that access requires it' (Independent Commission on Transport 1974: 260). They also pointed to the social injustice of the new car mobility which has put half the population who do not have regular use of a car at a serious disadvantage.

The commission's report was the first step in a movement to new philosophies of transport which seeks to find accommodation between social values and the motorized mobility. It is still in progress.

Chapter five
TRANSPORT PLANNING

The planning of transport is a highly complex process. It involves consideration of alternative and complementary transport systems – their operation, finance and infrastructure – and choosing the best combination suited to the needs of an area. It also has to be considered within the framework of spatial and land use planning, and the economic and social context of communities. Many new and complex techniques have been developed in recent years which have attempted to bring objectivity into transport decision-making. Quantification not only of transport movement but also of economic benefits has been a part of that process. The new methods have not gone unchallenged. Fellow experts have challenged the methodologies used as unsound, and a broader criticism has been that they seek to reduce to a technical pseudo-objective basis decisions which are essentially political. Much of the argument about road and airport building centred round the data used, the calculations applied by government officials, and whether the public should have access to them. The struggle over methodology therefore became part of the political process and the resolution of some of the problems was an essential part of the attempt to re-establish a consensus basis for future planning.

LAND USE PLANNING

Land use planning deals with the distribution of activities and their related structures in geographical space. For example, living activities involve houses, shops and schools and these must be sited in relationship to each other, and in relation to working patterns and to leisure pursuits. Their distribution must be linked by appropriate forms of transport which provide convenient access to them, whether by walking, bicycle, car, bus or train. These in turn will require pavements, cycle tracks and roads, as well as bus and train stations, garages and depots, and petrol filling stations.

The constraints on physical planning are the physical characteristics of the area in question and the existing structures. A river is a natural barrier to development which has to be taken into consideration. Existing housing which lies in the way of a projected new residential area is another limiting factor. Planning authorities have only limited powers: they cannot order facilities to be built, only provide the parameters within which development by other organizations and enterprises can take place. When these bodies are part of the same organization, the job is straightforward; e.g. a county council is both a planning and a transport authority and can therefore build the local roads which it puts into its county plan. But a shire county is not a housing authority and it is up to the county district councils to build the council houses for which the plan has made provision. Similarly, the county council relies on the National Bus Company to run buses on the roads for which it has planned, and British Rail to run rail services.

The physical planning process took its first comprehensive form in the Town and Country Planning Act, 1947, which required all county and county borough councils to prepare development plans for the future in relation to land use, and to revise them every five years. The Act also brought almost all individual developments under control by making them subject to planning permission by the same local authorities. The development plans which resulted clearly defined zones for housing, industry, parks and shops, and included sites for roads and airports. The 1968 Town and Country Planning Act replaced development plans by more flexible structure plans which outlined policies for land use in broad terms but without detailed map definition. It also required local authorities to include policies for transport and traffic management in their structure plans, as well as for the improvement of the physical environment. All county councils are responsible for structure plans, but the district councils and London boroughs also play two important roles: they may draw up local plans within the broad policy set out in the structure plans and they are responsible for nearly all development control.

The control of land use is very closely related to transport planning. For example, a policy of housing development in an area adjoining a large city dictates the need for roads and for commuter transport services to the city. The extent and type of transport will depend on the housing densities. Low density housing will not support a bus service as readily as high density housing where access is easier and the volume of traffic will make the service commercially viable. Industrial development will require facilities for freight transport, and commercial and shopping development will need public transport and car parking.

The tendency of local authorities to plan only for traffic management and roadbuilding prompted the requirement via the 1968 Transport Act for planning authorities to include all kinds of transport planning within their structure plans. Co-ordination was further promoted in 1973 by the requirement on all county councils to submit annual TPPs setting out their overall transport strategy and objectives together with proposals for expenditure. Plans for public transport are also the responsibility of county councils, either through their control of PTEs (the metropolitan counties) or the annual PTPs (the shire counties). The combination of structure plans, TPPs and PTPs has joined land use and transport planning firmly together at the county council level in a way which was never previously possible.

DEVELOPMENT OF TRANSPORT PLANNING METHODOLOGY

The methods used to reach decisions on transport planning have become steadily more complex and sophisticated over the years to meet the demands placed upon the planning process. For example, in order to plan the sites for factories and offices, it is desirable to forecast the future working population and its location. The planning of roads requires accurate forecasting of future patterns of movement and traffic volumes if adequate provision is to be secured. One of the problems associated with road planning in the 1960s and 1970s arose from the fact that it concentrated only on the estimate of road traffic flows, based on projected estimates of car ownership and use, and arrived at the crude conclusion that road space needed to be increased to accommodate the projected increase. Later, more complex analyses began to be made of the likely effects of traffic restraint, and the interaction with public transport services. The 'modal split' of travel preferences between cars, buses and trains, for example, became a prediction of some importance. Transport planning has now developed a complex technology and professional practice of its own, with mathematical models, sophisticated statistical methods and a jargon as incomprehensible to the layman as any other specialized practice, but which is now more capable than previously of providing planners and decision-makers with the information on the options available to them. However, forecasting and modelling are not perfectly developed tools; they are subject to errors in performance. They are also expensive in terms of skilled manpower and computer time.

Cost benefit analysis

The introduction of cost benefit analysis has been an important development in transport planning. Cost benefit analysis is an economic evaluation which assesses projects and proposed developments in terms of their costs in resources and their benefits in goods and services provided. It has developed because of the problem of assessing public expenditure proposals for collective needs in areas where direct charges are not made to cover costs and the market economy measurements of prices and profitability cannot therefore be made. The alternative to market choice was political choice, but politicians who asked for guidance beyond their own political instincts and preferences often received only strictly financial appraisals which balanced capital expenditure against a limited range of direct benefits, and could be given no guidance on the social benefits and costs. For example, the Beeching Report (British Railways Board 1963) examined only the financial viability of the various operations of British Rail and not the social benefits of unprofitable passenger services. Roadbuilding proposals, up to the 1960s, were appraised only on their capital costs, and not on the benefits of journey time saved, accidents avoided, and operating costs reduced.

The technique of cost benefit analysis is first to list the costs and benefits to be included in the assessment. These will not only include the capital costs of the project and the immediate benefits to be gained, but also the 'external' effects such as the cost of agricultural land resulting from a land take for roadbuilding, or the benefit resulting from reduced journey times. Once listed, costs and benefits are each allotted to a monetary value for assessment purposes and these are aggregated so that the *net* cost or benefit can be calculated. An annual rate of return on the proposed capital expenditure can then be calculated, or the costs and benefits of alternative proposals can be assessed in order to decide between them.

The first major cost benefit analysis for a roadbuilding proposal was the M1 study by Coburn, Beesley, and Reynolds (1960). It estimated the benefits the new motorway was likely to bring in terms of reduced journey time on the motorway itself and on other roads relieved of congestion by traffic diverted to the motorway. It also put a value on the assumed reduction of accidents. The M1 study did not, however, attempt to assess the value of environmental changes.

The Buchanan Report *Traffic in Towns* (1963) set out a cost benefit analysis technique to assess the value of road and other planning proposals. It listed environment, accessibility and cost as the three factors to be measured if alternative proposals were to be compared. These factors were assessed in relation to alternative town centre schemes prepared for Newbury. The study allotted arbitrary values to such environmental factors as safety, comfort, convenience and appearance in its assessment, as well as to factors associated with accessibility. By using the values to measure the benefits of the different schemes, the study set up a comparison between their benefits to balance against the financial costs.

Similar techniques were used for a public transport proposal in the Victoria Line cost benefit analysis carried out for London Transport (Foster and Beesley 1963). The study assessed the value of the social benefits which would result from the new line, namely the reduction in journey time and costs and the improved comfort and convenience of travellers, both for traffic diverted to the line and traffic remaining on other lines and transport systems. It also assessed the benefits of newly generated traffic. It discovered that the benefits accruing gave a 'social rate of return' of 11.3 per cent to set against the loss calculated from a purely financial appraisal. The earlier dismissal of the proposal to build the Victoria Line as unviable in commercial terms was therefore reversed and the line was built to become an economic success.

The most controversial use of cost benefit analysis was the attempt by the Roskill Commission on the third London Airport to measure the costs and benefits of alternative sites. The commission's report put the case for the technique in the following terms (1971; para 3.13).

> First if we were to eschew purely arbitrary and subjective judgements we saw no practical alternative to cost benefit analysis as a framework for studying the problems. Secondly we would be able to test the extent to which cost benefit analysis could be made to embrace some of the factors which we had to consider while remaining sceptical about the acceptability of some of the results . . . At least an attempt would be made to measure and value factors which are external to ordinary market transactions.

And again on the 'human problems' it argued (ibid: para. 3.15)

> Cost benefit analysis does not ignore them. It seeks so far as it can to assist in bringing all problems into their proper perspective. It provides a logical framework within which to assess all the effects flowing from a particular investment or planning decision. It tries to ensure that decisions are taken on the basis of people's individual values and choices as revealed by their behaviour rather than on the basis of the decision maker's own preferences or standards or those of vociferous and politically powerful groups.

The commission's justification for cost-benefit analysis was both as a method of decision-making and as a technique of measurement. Although it opted out of trying to measure the visual value of landscape, it did seek to assess the noise costs of the proposed sites for the airport for comparison purposes as

> ... the sum of money required to restore the satisfaction of the residents to the level which was obtained before the noise nuisance was imposed upon them. The size of this loss is determined by reference to the effect of noise on house prices and by reference to survey data designed to show what value people attach to their homes over and above the market price. (ibid: para. 12.27.)

The commission's approach was strongly attacked, partly no doubt because the prospect of a gigantic third London Airport in a rural area was so repugnant to many that any method used to compare alternative sites was unacceptable. But there were also grave doubts as to whether environmental features like noise and visual disturbance could be measured by the market mechanism of financial loss and, even if they could, whether they could be aggregated and compared directly with measurements of other costs such as travel time, the redeployment of defence establishments or freight user costs. Finally, the claims of cost benefit analysis to provide a basis for 'rational' decision-making has been challenged by critics such as Peter Self (1975) as over-ambitious at best, or even an attempt to subvert political choice by substituting a pseudo-objective and by no means value-free bureaucratic process. Buchanan's note of dissent to the commission's report put the case against it more simply: 'I have the feeling that the whole cost benefit approach has been pushed too far and too fast beyond the fairly easily quantified problems that are its usual domain.'

Opposition to roadbuilding proposals on environmental grounds escalated in the 1970s and objectors effectively challenged not only the schemes but the arguments and methodology used to justify them. The Advisory Committee on Trunk Road Assessment (Chairman Sir George Leitch) was set up by the Department of Transport to defuse the situation by examining the methods of appraisal used. Its report of 1977 endorsed the framework used in assessment based on forecasting and cost benefit analysis. It set out five criteria for assessments: they should be comprehensible, comprehensive, inexpensive, provide for a rational balance of factors and recognize the groups of people who were affected. But it found that 'It is unsatisfactory that the assessment should be so dominated by those factors which are susceptible to valuation in money terms and we believe it to be inadequate to rely simply on a checklist to comprehend environmental factors' (Leitch Report 1977).

The Leitch Report made a series of recommendations designed to improve assessment. On forecasting methods, it recommended moving away from extrapolatory techniques, which simply based future trends on past ones, and toward a 'causal' model which identified the factors likely to cause change and incorporated them as variables. Car ownership would thus be forecast not on the basis of past growth but according to changes in such factors as household income and structure, the density of residential population, the costs of car ownership and the availability of public transport services. It found the computer-based cost-benefit analysis system used by the Department of Transport for roads (known as COBA) to be basically satisfactory, but suggested certain improvements. The report was more critical of the assessment made of environmental and other non-economic factors and proposed several changes. Noise disturbance, which was measured only in relation to individual properties of different types, should be described in a more general way by the use of 'before and after' noise contour maps. Land losses should include not only the money value of land which had to be acquired but also a grading according to its agricultural value. Urban schemes should attempt to assess time savings and possibly also disturbance for pedestrians. All schemes should assess the effects on car drivers' comfort and convenience. Although the report was anxious to see the direct effects of road schemes on local employment included (e.g. where a road gave access to a factory site), it was very doubtful about the effects on future economic development, and thought these should be included only where strong evidence could be provided. Finally, it urged that similar techniques of appraisal should be used to compare roadbuilding and other transport system investment proposals for the purposes of policy decisions at a strategic level.

The government promised to re-examine its assessment procedures in the light of the Leitch Report. In 1978, Sir George Leitch was asked to chair a Standing Advisory Committee on Trunk Road Assessment in order to advise on the changes that were needed. Some of these lay outside the Department of Transport's exclusive competence. For example, the recommendation for some standardization of the evaluation methods used for urban road schemes required the co-operation of the local authorities responsible for them. In the 1980 White Paper *Policy for Roads: England 1980*, Cmnd 7908, it was reported that traffic forecasting has been modified to include the causal model recommended by the report on car ownership. But the White Paper, like the Transport Policy White Paper of 1977 continued to argue the general case for roadbuilding as an aid to economic development.

SURVEY TECHNIQUES – THE CONSUMER APPROACH

A different approach to the measurement of people's reactions to planning proposals involves the use of survey and interview techniques. Cost benefit analysis, as has been shown, came under severe criticism as a way of measuring consumer preferences through monetary values. Another method, involving consultation and 'public participation', which developed from the stimulus provided by the Skeffington Report, attempted to assess public reactions to planning proposals by inviting public comment. It, too, was criticized for its doubtful representative quality. Survey techniques and household interviews have been developed in an attempt to identify the values and priorities that people attach to the different features of transport plans. They signify an important shift towards a consumer-based approach. The priority evaluation scheme developed by Social and Community Planning Research, for example, first assessed the importance people attached to environmental factors such as low traffic noise and to accessibility factors such as journey time to work. It then asked respondents to trade-off gains against losses and arrive at a choice or preference which balanced the two (Hoinville 1977). Stephen Plowden pushes the idea of consumer choice forward as the basis of future transport planning. Surveys should be used to discover how people travel, what problems they encounter and what improvements they would appreciate. These would form the bases for transport proposals within financial and other constraints (Plowden 1980).

Similar techniques are employed by the Household Activity –

Travel Simulator (HATS) as a check on the real-life reactions to transport plans (Jones 1979; 1980). It involves the use of display equipment which provides information on the basis of which a series of loosely structured interviews takes place. The interviewees in the HATS survey are asked to identify how they would adapt their behaviour to different transport or land use proposals. The results from this kind of survey can be used as a check on mathematical modelling forecasts or to evaluate the effect of various policy options. By providing information which is a more realistic reflection of actual behaviour than the formal statistical exercises, the technique allows transport planners to present options whose effects can be predicted with a greater degree of certainty than previously. At the same time, they do not attempt to quantify reactions in money terms or to trade them off against other types of gain and loss.

Attempts to measure, to refine calculations of all kinds through sophisticated methods and to use survey techniques are thus continually developing. But human reactions do not wait on improved methodology and can escalate into political expression which affects the decisions made in a very old-fashioned way. Interest groups reflecting both economic self-interest and broader social concerns have been both active and effective in influencing government policy decisions in the last two decades. Their activity and influence is described in the chapter which follows.

Part two
POLITICS AND POLICIES

Chapter six

PRESSURE GROUPS AND THE PUBLIC

INTEREST AND PRESSURE GROUPS

Transport is both a major industry and a vital consumer concern. As an industry it covers a wide range of activities from the operation of passenger and freight transport services, to the manufacture of vehicles, equipment, buildings and track, roads or runways. Its impact on the public is direct, immediate and perceptible. Transport services are a key part of everyday life and of the operations of all types of business ranging from mining and agriculture, through to manufacturing and retailing. A strike by petrol tanker drivers can bring the economy to a standstill; late trains or buses can wreck daily routines; a rise in transport costs can affect the profitability of a firm; public contracts for roads and bridges are vital to many civil engineering firms; the sight, noise and fumes of lorries or aircraft can wreck an otherwise pleasant environment; the congestion or speed of motor traffic can make everyday city life for cyclists and pedestrians a dangerous and fearful experience. It is not therefore surprising that there are a large number of trade associations, users' and residents' groups in the transport scene, as well as a wide range of environmental and civic societies seeking to influence transport policy. There are substantial links between the various groups: the trade associations join with user groups to form pressure groups, and pressure group membership overlaps with societies whose members do not have a direct personal or economic interest. The broader groupings centre round the roadbuilders and users, ranging from motorists, road haulage and freight interests to asphalt and concrete manufacturers on the one hand, and the public transport (especially railways) operators and users, the civic societies and the environmentalists on the other. However, the divisions are not always clear-cut. Bus operators, for example, have an interest in roads but also in public transport which is usually associated with the environmentalist cause and railways have an interest in freight carriage. Exceptionally, elements from both groups will unite for an overall objective, as in the case of the representations made to government for an increase in investment in all kinds of transport in 1981.

Not all the interest groups are permanent. Often as issues arise, local residents have formed together in associations to put forward their views and protect their interests. In developing campaigns, they may join together with other similar groups and with more permanent organizations which have a stake in the issue or are sympathetic to their cause. Where the question is one which affects a wide area dozens of groups may be involved. Some forty voluntary associations gave evidence to the Roskill Commission on the third London Airport (Report of the Commission 1971). Among them, one of the five resistance organizations which were federations of many smaller societies, was the Wing Airport Resistance Association (WARA) which had 15 town and 188 village groups affiliated to it and was supported by some 46 other societies, including local branches of the Women's Institute and the Council for the Protection of Rural England (CPRE), gardening and allotment associations and a federation of local pigeon fanciers (Kimber and Richardson 1974b).

The established national lobby and pressure groups often started as scratch organizations, put together to meet an immediate challenge. The BRF emerged from a conference convened in 1932 to prepare evidence which would combat the views of the railways lobby. It stayed in being and after 1945 became the protagonist on behalf of many organizations for the roadbuilding cause. The National Council on Inland Transport was formed to fight the Beeching rail cuts of 1963 and is still in being. Transport 2000 was formed in 1972 with the backing of the rail unions to promote the rail cause, and has since developed into a pressure group for all forms of public transport and one of several national organizations allied to the environmental movement. The picture is a complex one, notable for its richness and variety. The twenty years since the publication of the Buchanan and Beeching Reports has been marked by a period of exceptional political activity in the area of transport, both by trade and economic interests and through 'a remarkable flowering of voluntary group activity whose purpose is to complement, or improve, the quality of public services by representing the interests of those who consume the service, or are affected by it' (Sharpe 1975a).

The politics of transport

To disentangle the various skeins, it is useful to divide the organizations into sectional interest groups, i.e. trade groups with a direct commercial interest to protect; private user and residents' groups, i.e. those directly affected by transport proposals; promotional groups appealing to public interest issues; and political campaigning groups either directly associated with either of these or with an interest arising from their general concerns. There are also instances of new political parties formed to put up candidates for election with transport issues as the key or an important part of their platform.

SECTIONAL INTEREST GROUPS

Trade associations

Nearly all trades have a user interest in transport services because of the need to assemble the components for their operations and to distribute the final product. The trades with a direct interest in surface transport are those concerned with the manufacture and sale of vehicles, with the manufacture of transport track, and with the operation of services. The Society of Motor Manufacturers and Traders is an umbrella organization for the motor vehicle industry, founded in 1902 and with a present membership of over 1,500 firms, covering a very broad spectrum from Rolls Royce to engineering and rubber manufacturing concerns. The Motor Agents' Association and the Scottish Motor Trade Association cover the service stations, garages and car sellers. The associations involved in roadbuilding and surfacing who depend on government, both central and local, for their contracts, include the British Aggregate Construction Materials Industries, formed in 1982 from the Cement and Concrete, Asphalt and Coated Macadam, Sand and Gravel and other associations. A former director of the British Road Federation heads the giant association's staff. Among the operators, the principal associations are the RHA representing professional road hauliers which has a membership of over 14,000 firms, and the FTA many of whose 16,000 members operate road transport services as an ancillary part of their main trade concerns. Bus and coach operators are organized into the Confederation of Public Road Passenger Transport Associations. The London Taxi Drivers run their own association. The RIA acts for the manufacturers of railway equipment of all kinds and the Barge and Canal Development

Association represents the interests of those involved in commercial canal operations.

The various trade associations all make representations to government on their immediate trade interests and many are represented on the CBI's Transport Committee. They combine together in common campaigns, the most important of which is for road-building and improvement where the relevant associations combine to finance the BRF. The railway and canal associations on the other hand are part of Transport 2000 which puts the case for railway and waterborne traffic. Business and trade association interests are represented through the *Transport Policy Committee of the CBI* which has a rotating membership appointed for a three-year period of some thirty members. Included in 1982 were the important trade associations (SMMT, RHA, FTA, the British Shippers' Council) the chief transport operators (British Rail, BA, National Bus Company, British Caledonian Airways), important transport users (The Post Office, Marks and Spencer, ICI, Freeman's Mail Order) and manufacturers (British Aerospace, Tarmac). The committee's comprehensive membership means that it must often seek an accommodation between competing interests in its policy recommendations. It is clear in its advocacy of greater public expenditure on all kinds of transport infrastructure and a transport system which is 'market-orientated' and it advocates a similar approach to the analysis of all transport investment projects, whether for road, rail or water, for purposes of comparison. While it broadly opposes general subsidies for both passenger and freight transport, it is aware of the importance to business of good commuter services. Overall, it stresses the need to give priority to 'wealth-producing' rather than 'socially desirable' expenditure in the transport area. For that reason it puts economic considerations before social and environmental measures in its transport priorities, and favours the raising of limits on lorry weights as a measure which will reduce transport costs and make industry more competitive.

Trade unions

The trade unions whose members provide transport services are the Transport and General Workers' Union (TGWU) (road haulage, buses, airlines and airports), the National Union of Railwaymen (NUR), the Associated Society of Locomotive Engineers and Firemen (ASLEF) and the Transport Salaried Staffs' Association (railways) (TSSA) and the British Airline Pilots' Association (BAPA).

Because the unions work to separate trades, their campaigning interests are sometimes split into opposing camps. Thus the TGWU has tended to support the lorry and road interest, while the NUR, ASLEF, and TSSA support rail. They combine to support the nationalized transport operators and to promote public transport, an integrated transport policy and increased levels of investment into all transport services.

Local branches of trade unions have been involved in transport campaigns, especially when public transport is threatened. A London Trades Union Defence Committee was formed to back the GLC's 'Keep Fares Fair' campaign in 1982, and the transport unions had supported the earlier 'Save our Public Transport Services' campaign in London in 1977. Employment prospects are a key factor in trade union support. In 1967 for example, the Harlow and Stansted Trades Council supported the Stansted Airport proposal for that reason (Jay 1980).

The Trades Union Congress concerns itself with transport policy. In 1956, for example, it unanimously agreed that the roadbuilding programme was inadequate and pressed for a bigger one, but by 1965 it was concerned to subordinate commitments on urban motorway expenditure to a consideration of the priorities to be accorded to private and public transport, and in 1975 it was urging restraint on cars in urban centres. The TUC has consistently put the case for an integrated transport system which would, along Morrisonian lines, co-ordinate the rail and road services. In 1965 it wanted to see the BTC reconstituted as the co-ordinating body, and in 1975 its Transport Industries Committee pressed for a new national body to carry out the function of co-ordination. The proposal for an advisory National Transport Council in the government's 1976 Consultation Document was a response to this pressure but was not implemented. The TUC in 1981 advocated the setting up of a National Transport Planning Authority to plan and co-ordinate transport investment. The recent privatization of bus and airline services and of the National Freight Corporation has been opposed by the TUC. The TUC does not take a clear line on environmental issues. For example, it currently accepts the case for expanding Stansted Airport. But it is opposed to an increase in maximum permitted lorry weights and for a stronger research programme into environmentally acceptable lorries. The TUC's support for public transport, with greater investment including rail electrification, and more resources devoted to subsidies, allies it with an important part of the environmentalists' case.

User groups

The motoring organizations. These may be included as a sectional interest because of the important economic interest that motorists have in using their cars for commuting and work purposes. The Automobile Association (AA) has over 5 m. members and the Royal Automobile Club (RAC) has between 1 m. and 2 m.

The RAC was formed as a members' club in 1897 to promote 'automobilism' and to encouraged the motor industry once the old restrictions which obliged all 'light locomotives' on the roads to be preceded by a man on foot bearing a red flag had been abolished. Motoring was a pastime of the wealthy amateur interested in the technology of the new vehicles as well as the excursions they provided. The club atmosphere suited the age, but soon the members were in trouble with the police, particularly in rural areas, for exceeding the 20 mph speed limit. Police traps were set for speeding motorists and to combat them a new and more militant group was formed in 1905, which became the AA. Both associations grew with car ownership and the motoring public. Their breakdown service has always been an enormous attraction and in 1976 was reckoned by 98 per cent of the AA's members surveyed to be one of its three most important services, along with legal defence and the relay (collection) service (Barty-King 1980). Since 1945 they have diversified their activities into insurance, technical inspection, travel services and publishing.

Both organizations have also continued to see their role as 'protecting the interest of the motorist' and run sections devoted to the consideration of public policy which, separately and in alliance with each other and with trade interests, lobby MPs and the government and run public campaigns. Their Standing Joint Committee exists to present a united view. One continuing campaign has been for an expanded roadbuilding programme. The basic view of the organizations may be summarized in the AA's submission to the secretary of state in 1976

> The Automobile Association is a firm believer in the future of the motor vehicle and particularly of the motor car in Britain's motorised society. Because of the enormous accumulated private investment in the motor car running into many thousands of million pounds it must be in the country's interest economically to encourage its use and not to discourage it. (1976: 1)

The AA therefore urged that 'a firm programme of inter-city and urban route construction should be established and adhered to', and that public transport services should meet their costs, or be withdrawn. The RAC also takes a strong line against compulsory seat belts and the 'excessive burden' of motoring taxation.

It is difficult to know to what extent the motoring organizations represent, as they claim, the views of 'motorists'. The RAC is still very much a private club with premises in Pall Mall for its full members and with associate members restricted to its road services. The AA as a company is in theory accountable at an annual general meeting, but makes no provision for gathering its members' views which it seeks to represent on public policy issues. As a group, car owners are now less distinguishable than before as 'motorists'. Many use their cars as they would any other piece of domestic machinery; the cost, wear and traffic conditions concern them but they do not see themselves as having an identifiable group interest any more than they would as the users of washing machines. The motoring associations have probably declined in influence from the early days when their technical advice and co-operation was valued by government and they wielded important political influence.

Freight users are represented in the *Freight Transport Association*, which combines the representation of firms who use freight transport with those who operate their own lorry fleets as a subsidiary part of their business. The FTA is a large and powerful organization which has regular contacts with government departments and MPs. It opposed the introduction of the tachograph, supports new road construction which will yield economic benefits, favours heavier lorries and higher speed limits for them on the motorways, and opposes 'ill-conceived' lorry bans. It favours 'freedom of choice' for freight transport users but wants to see the maximum use of rail freight services consistent with service and cost competitiveness.

Public transport users. A number of local groups using public transport have been formed, often as users of a particular service, or within one locality. Of the first type, the North London Line Committee and the Southend Rail Users' Association are examples. The second kind include local groups like the Hackney Public Transport Campaign and the Harrow Public Transport Users' Association, and larger groupings like the London Passengers' Action Federation and The National Association of Railway Passengers. These groups have the important function of representing user interests to the transport operators, to their planning and controlling bodies, and to the statutory consumer committees. Some are also affiliated to wider transport interest groups, such as the National Council on Inland Transport and the London Amenity and Transport Association (LATA). They appear naturally in campaigns for better and cheaper public transport, such as the 1977 London 'Save our Public Transport Services' and the 1982 GLC-backed campaign for subsidized fares.

The *Inland Waterways Association* is a thriving group with over 19,000 individual members in 1980 which campaigns for the restoration of more canals and their use for both freight and recreation purposes. It held a national rally in 1980, sells maps, canal guides and histories and represents the users' viewpoint to the British Waterways Board and the Department of the Environment.

There are a number of cyclists' organizations. The oldest, the *Cyclists' Touring Club* formed in 1878 was one of the founder organizations of the Roads Improvement Association in 1886, set up to campaign for better road surfaces. The CTC is today a member of the CPRE and Transport 2000.

The small *Pedestrians' Association*, formed in 1929 has focused attention on road safety and the rights of pedestrians. It has campaigned for lower speed limits and their stricter enforcement. Pavement parking and other obstructions to pedestrians is another current cause for concern.

Journeys by cycle and foot are an important part of leisure and recreation, particularly in the country, and recreational groups take a strong interest in transport affairs. The *Ramblers' Association*, for example, is affiliated to the CPRE, Transport 2000 and the Council for Environmental Conservation (CoEnCo) and the Youth Hostels' Association is affiliated to CPRE and CoEnCo.

Finally, although women cannot be considered as a special class of transport user, the presence of women's organizations affiliated to a number of user groups and in various campaigns is notable. The *National Federation of Women's Institutes* and the *National Union of Townswomen's Guilds*, for example, both belong to Transport 2000 and the former to CPRE. Women's Institute branches have been active in numerous local campaigns, e.g. the WARA, the M3 Action Group, and in London the Women's Fares Fight Campaign Group formed in 1982. The greater reliance of women on public transport and walking as transport modes is no doubt one reason for this participation.

Local and residents' groups

The last important groups which can be said to have a direct sectional interest are the local and residents' groups campaigning to protect the interest of a community which feels itself threatened by transport proposals or operations. Some of these may be old-established civic societies, while others are community protection groups newly formed in the face of particular proposals. Often, the two types of society join together for stronger campaigning. In Bedford, for example, in 1970, proposals for a new river crossing were opposed both by the well-established Bedford Society and by a newly formed group called 'Crisis' (Blowers 1980). The London Motorway Action Group (LMAG) in 1971 included four civic societies as well as eight residents' associations, thirteen action groups, two ratepayers' associations, and one property owners' association. Another allied body, LATA, had seventeen civic societies affiliated plus numerous residents' associations (LMAG and LATA 1971). In York, the Civic Trust played an important part in the negotiations over the creation of a pedestrian precinct in 1971 and in subsequent discussions over the ring road (Palliser 1974). The Winchester Society was part of the M3 Action Group (Dowse and Hughes 1977).

If the established societies often formed the nucleus of local action groups, the determination and speed with which new committees were formed is also noteworthy. For example, in Portsmouth in 1967 and Southampton in 1968 residents' associations were formed to combat road plans (Grant 1977). As consideration of a line for the proposed M4 proceeded in the 1960s, associations sprang up to protect each proposed route (Gregory 1974). As the government announced in 1979 its reconsideration (again!) of six inland sites for the third London Airport, earlier resistance committees disbanded in 1971 were quickly reconstituted (Buchanan 1981). When the Lords' decision made fares subsidies for London Transport illegal in 1981, a 'Fares Fight' campaign sprang up separately from the GLC's own 'Keep Fares Fair' campaign with groups in some twenty London boroughs.

Although local councillors and local political parties were sometimes associated with the groups, they have been remarkable for their independence from the established political machinery. Formed for a cause, and able to draw on widespread support from individuals and a variety of local organizations and to raise substantial funds, they just as quickly disbanded once the work was done.

PROMOTIONAL OR PUBLIC INTEREST GROUPS

The broad range of public interest or promotional groups whose members do not have a direct economic or commercial interest in the cause they espouse includes a number of national organizations which take a strong interest in transport matters.

The *Civic Trust*, for example, is a national organization devoted to the protection and improvement of the environment which has some 1,000 local groups on its registers. Much of its work has to do with the encouragement of projects of architectural restoration and landscape conservation and improvement. But it has consistently made a strong stand in favour of restraint of heavy lorries and against increased lorry weights and has queried the usefulness of by-passes as a remedial measure. It helped to form Transport 2000 in 1972. The civic societies vary greatly in strength and activity. An unusual society, outside the general mould, is the *London Amenity and Transport Association*, which is characterized by its strong links with professional planners in the transport field. LATA was set up in 1967 by a group of planners at the London School of Economics including J. M. Thomson and S. Plowden. It was intended as a federation of civic and amenity organizations which would work with the GLC and the Department of Transport for 'rational' policies (Thomson 1977). It became involved in the struggle against the motorways in the Greater London Development Plan, and provided the intellectual backing and expertise through which the proposals were effectively challenged. It continues to campaign on London issues and runs on minimal funding from its affiliated local societies.

Another organization with a broad remit, the *Council for the Protection of Rural England* (founded 1926) has branches in forty-four counties, and a variety of constituent bodies which include the local authority associations, the professional institutes of architects, surveyors and town planners, several recreation associations, nature and conservation societies, and women's, farmers' and landowners' groups. The CPRE is strongly against the raising of limits on lorry weights. It opposes the choice of Stansted as the third London Airport and queries the need for a further international airport.

Societies concerned with the conservation of natural resources have also become involved with transport issues. *The Conservation Society*, formed in 1966, advocates policies which will restrain the growth of traffic and discriminate in favour of transport modes which cause the least damage to the environment and have the smallest consumption of energy and other resources. It therefore favours rail travel and policies which assist walking and cycling, and advocates a comparative analysis of proposals for all transport modes on the same objective basis.

Friends of the Earth and *Ecology groups* attached to the main political parties are similarly involved. Another group of societies with transport interests are concerned with health, noise and clean air: the National Society for Clean Air, the Local Authorities Aircraft Noise Council and the newly formed Campaign for Lead-Free Air (CLEAR) have clear involvements. Indeed, the large number of societies with allied aims and interests led to the founding of an umbrella organization, CoEnCo for more effective co-ordination of their work.

What is remarkable is the way in which these well-established societies have joined together to campaign on transport matters. Such involvement illustrates the central significance of transport in so many aspects of modern society, and especially its effects on the physical environment.

LOBBY AND PRESSURE GROUPS

There is no clear line between the sectional and promotional interest groups and the lobbyists. All the groups described earlier lobby at the political level when they wish to defend and promote their interests. However, a number have joined together to form organizations specifically designed as lobbying and propaganda organizations to influence government and opinion-forming groups and in some cases to campaign among the general public. In transport affairs the lobby has coalesced round two main groupings: the combination of trade interests, industrial and other road users campaigning for roadbuilding and the raising of weight restrictions on lorries; and an amalgamation of environment, civic and local residents' societies, plus railway and canal trade interests campaigning against new roads and larger and heavier lorries and for the promotion of public transport.

The British Road Federation. Agitation for the improvement of roads to take motor vehicles goes back to the last years of the nineteenth century. At that time, the need was for resurfacing which would make roads more suitable for traffic and restrict dust. The Roads Improvement Association, founded in 1886 by two cyclists' organizations, was joined by the new motor car enthusiasts in 1901

Table 6.1 Pressure groups – membership and finances

Organization	Year	Membership (individual)	Areal organization	Affiliated membership	Annual income (£)
Road Haulage Association	1980		14 area offices	14,117 firms	1,048,879
Freight Transport Association	1980		5 regional offices	16,000 firms	3,600,000
British Road Federation	1981		2 regional offices	50+ trade associations, etc.	300,000
Inland Waterways Association	1980	19,274	7 regional offices, 30 branches		146,033
Pedestrians' Association	1980	750		50 societies	5,628
Ramblers' Association	1980–81	37,027	6 local branches	508 clubs 195 groups	187,015
Transport 2000	1981		35 local groups	28 affiliated organizations	25,000
Council for the Protection of Rural England	1980	30,000	43 branches and county associations	33 constituent bodies	100,977
Conservation Society	1979–80	5,908	39 branches		29,944

The politics of transport

to put the case for an improved system of administering and financing roads. The solution found in 1909 was for the financing of road improvements by taxes on vehicles and on petrol administered through a Road Fund and Road Board. In spite of the agitation of the Roads Improvement Association, the road fund was gradually reabsorbed into general revenues and finally lost its independence in 1937. The struggle for more funding for roads was carried on by the Standing Joint Committee of the AA and RAC.

The BRF had been founded in 1932 from a conference of road interests with the intention of combating the viewpoint of the railways. It came strongly to the forefront of the roadbuilding campaign with its publication *Britain's Roads – a new deal* in 1954 and helped to form the Roads Campaign Council in 1955 together with the RHA, the SMMT, AA and RAC and three bus operators' associations. It was already described in 1958 as 'the chief propagandist body in this field' (Finer 1958). The Roads Campaign Council set a target for a ten-year roadbuilding programme costing £750 m. Lobbying work at the level of Parliament and the 'opinion leaders' were carried out by the BRF, and its campaign to the public through the organization 'Aims for Industry'. The BRF briefed MPs and sent groups of them off to Western Europe to see the new motorways there. It formed an all-party roads study group for MPs. It held conferences, published studies and statistics and ran regional campaigns. *Aims for Industry* mounted a 'Road Crusade' in 1956 and sent a mobile show of exhibitions and films to twenty-four towns round the country, collecting half a million signatures to its petition for more and better roads.

The BRF is acknowledged as a very strong lobby within Parliament and with local councillors, with good access to civil servants in the Department of Transport and the TRRL (Hamer 1974). In 1981, its annual budget exceeded £300,000, and it employed a staff of sixteen people in London, with small regional offices in Manchester and the Midlands. In its last published annual report of 1976, the BRF listed fifty-six member organizations, of which about half had direct interests in road construction, haulage and motor vehicles and half represented a variety of industries using transport. The most prominent organizations included the AA and RAC, the RHA, the SMMT, the National Bus Company, the FTA and the National Chamber of Trade.

The BRF continues to use tried and proven methods of influencing public policy. In 1976 it reported that it had written to the top 1,000 industrial companies urging them to put their views to government on the 1976 Transport Consultation Paper, had serviced the all-party Roads Study Group of the House of Commons, and had set up five 'working lunches' for groups of MPs and arranged two study tours for them. It had also campaigned for over fifty highway schemes through its nine regional groups in 1976 and in some cases helped neighbouring highway authorities to promote co-ordinated schemes. The target was the completion of 4,500 miles of motorways and trunk roads by about 1990, plus a basic network of high-standard roads and 'sensible traffic management' in towns. Through a new pressure group, Movement for London, it had also joined with the London Taxidriver's Association in a campaign in 1976 against the 'indiscriminate' introduction of bus lanes by the GLC.

The BRF has opposed subsidies to railways but maintains that it is not anti-rail but is there to secure adequate road networks. Although rail and road interests have tended to group in opposing camps, the present cutbacks in all transport investment have unusually brought them together and have prompted a novel campaign by the BRF in alliance with British Rail and the unions representing both road and railway workers. In 1981, there was a joint appeal to the government to reverse the downward trend in transport investment of all kinds and to raise it to a minimum of 1 per cent of gross domestic product.

As regards road haulage and the issue of maximum lorry weights, the BRF has argued for the building of motorways as a way of diverting heavy lorries from less suitable roads in residential, shopping and rural areas where they cause environmental disturbance. It favours the EEC proposals to increase permitted lorry weights because of the saving in energy and freight costs and opposes any subsidies or measures of direction to transfer freight to rail. The BRF has not, however, become involved in other issues affecting motorists or lorry owners and drivers such as tachographs and safety belts.

Transport 2000. Transport 2000 was founded in 1972 on the initiative of the NUR which convened a conference of the railway unions, the environmental societies and the RIA to conduct a campaign for an integrated transport policy and a larger role for the railways (Bagwell 1982). Sidney Weighell was its first secretary but it had no paid director or individual membership. In 1977, after Sir Peter Parker became chairman, British Rail took the decision to give financial support to Transport 2000 which has since had a small permanent office and staff. It has now become a lobby in favour of public transport, especially rail, and for the provision of improved facilities for cyclists and pedestrians and against heavier lorries.

The twenty-eight organizations affiliated to Transport 2000 are an unusually broad mixture of civic and environmental groups and transport users, combined with operators, unions and trade associations. Half are promotional groups, varying from the environmental societies such as the Ancient Monuments Society, the CPRE and the Civic Trust to the conservationists (Conservation Society), and ecologists (Friends of the Earth). British Rail and the three railway unions provide a solid rail input, reinforced by the major sectional interests, the RIA representing manufacturers of railway rolling stock and equipment and the Barge and Canal Development Association. Non-motorist user groups (the Cyclists' Touring Club and Ramblers' Association) are joined by two women's groups (the Women's Institutes and Townswomen's Guilds, both at national level). There are also three political groups, (the Conservative and Liberal ecology groups and the Socialist Environmental and Resources Association).

Like its counterpart the BRF, Transport 2000 is an umbrella organization for a variety of interests and lobbies MPs and local councillors, makes representations to the Department of Transport, publishes a monthly newsheet and encourages research projects. The contrast with the BRF lies in the resources available; the annual income of Transport 2000 is £25,000 and it employs only three people in its national office. The development of Transport 2000 in the 1970s to an effective lobbying organization has been the result of the big upsurge of interest in public transport and in environmental issues. While many of its constituent organizations lobby separately on aspects of transport policy of particular interest to them, it provides a common platform on which public transport advocates, conservationists and environmentalists can broadly agree.

The National Council on Inland Transport was formed to fight the rail cuts in 1963 and to promote public transport facilities. Its membership partly replicates Transport 2000 as both include the rail unions and the RIA. The National Council also has some thirty-five local authorities in membership and several public transport user groups, but it does not include British Rail or the environmental groups. It has no full-time staff and very modest financial resources.

The Council for Environmental Conservation was set up in 1969 as a central agency to co-ordinate the work of conservation and environmental organizations. Its transport committee brings together many of the organizations previously listed whose views it furthers.

The *Green Alliance* is a new information and lobbying organization set up in 1978 by the Dartington Trust. The alliance has a radical ecological viewpoint on transport as on other matters. It is aimed largely at MPs and it publishes a parliamentary newsletter.

In terms of organization, the BRF clearly has a unity and single-mindedness which its opponents with a proliferation of organizations lack. The problem seems to be that while the BRF has one overriding aim – more roads – the other side has a lot of broad objectives, and is often clearer about what it does *not* want – more roads, heavier lorries and new airports – than what it does want. 'A good environment' is an aspiration rather than a programme. More and better public transport is the clearest single aim put forward which can be pressed on government, while the package of conservation measures and the radical ecological viewpoint is less identifiable, comprehensible and probably less publicly acceptable. The breadth of their aims is reflected in the wide membership of the organizations. While the BRF has a solid membership of sectional interests plus the motorists' organizations, their opponents – Transport 2000, CoEnCo, the CPRE and the NCIT – have largely the same members in different combinations and permutations (see Fig. 6.1). For example, the Ramblers' Association, the Civic Trust and the IWA belong to three each (but not the same three). Also, bewilderingly, the National Council for Inland Transport and CPRE belong to Transport 2000 and they sit on CoEnCo's transport committee, but Transport 2000 is only an observer on the latter. It is possible to argue that the breadth of the organizations, their many affiliations and their local branches add to the leverage they exert and reflect their grass roots strength. But it can also be concluded that the compact and singleminded BRF is a more effective organization for lobbying purposes, certainly at departmental and probably also at parliamentary level.

The diversity and wide spread of local societies can, however, work to advantage on particular issues. The big campaigns which can mobilize strong support from local groups are able to bring the kind of pressure to bear on government and Parliament which is effective. The impressively large numbers of local societies affiliated to the LMAG and LATA in 1971, e.g. in their campaign against the London motorways, influenced the political parties. The Lon-

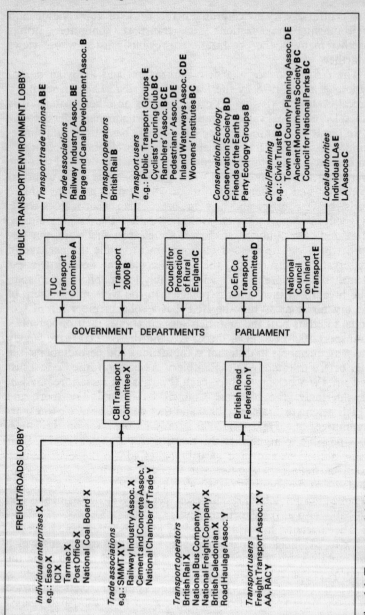

Fig. 6.1 Transport lobbies

don Labour Party, which had supported the ringway road proposals in 1966, was converted to an anti-motorways stand in the 1973 GLC elections, so that even when the Layfield Inquiry recommended in favour of Ringway One in December 1972, its proposal was a dead duck in political terms when Labour won the election in May 1973.

ELECTION CAMPAIGNS

The campaigning and lobbying groups operate at the level of officials, ministers, local councillors and MPs. They have their groups of 'friendly' MPs and councillors who can be relied on to ask questions and put forward points in committee from a brief supplied by the organization. They seek to influence a wider spectrum of elected representatives through newsletters, conferences and other activities: the BRF's all-party roads study group and their regional groups and conferences are models of competent activity in this respect. But they carefully stay clear of commitment to any one political party, even if they know that most of their support comes from one rather than the others.

It is when compaigning groups decide that the issue is too urgent to leave to the slower process of conversion to their policy of existing political parties, or when they find the parties incorrigibly unreceptive, that moves are made to put forward distinctive political candidates. One interesting instance was the *'Homes before Roads'* campaign in the 1970 GLC elections. In 1970 the Conservatives in control on the GLC were pressing ahead with their motorway proposals. The GLC Labour Group, which had supported motorway plans in 1966, had switched its stand against Ringway One in 1969 and was supported by the Regional Conference of the Party, but there was still a pro-motorway group among the councillors (said to be led by Ted Castle). At this time Labour's stance was described as 'sceptical but a little ambiguous' (Jay 1980). The LMAG was anxious to remain a broadly-based non-political campaigning group, but a group of its members saw the opportunity to present a clear case to the electorate in the 1970 GLC elections. 'Homes before Roads' was a scratch political campaign, organized by some of the leading lights of the LMAG and LATA, under the title name of the London Coalition. In two months, it put forward candidates standing for a policy to scrap the Greater London Development Plan, abandon the motorways and devote the resources freed to building and improving housing and to improving public transport services. The 73 candidates polled 71,121 votes and their action sharpened the attention of the existing parties to the growing opposition to the motorways.

Another example of separate political campaigning is the *Ecology Party*, founded in 1973, which has put up candidates at national, local and European elections. One of its important planks is a policy which reduces the dependence on transport, and encourages those forms of transport which use fuel most efficiently and conserve resources. It therefore favours cheap public transport, the use of railways and canals for freight and opposes major roadbuilding. The Ecology Party in 1982 had some 4,000 members in 200 local branches. Its 53 parliamentary candidates in 1979 polled on average 1.5 per cent of all the votes cast. It has had more success with local council candidates – some 300 stood for the county council elections of 1981, some received up to 10 per cent of the votes and one was elected in Cornwall. The Ecology Party has close links with the thriving Green and Radical parties in the EEC countries.

THE LOBBIES AND THE DEPARTMENT OF TRANSPORT

One of the disturbing features of the immediate past years has been the increasing distrust of the Department of Transport's work and allegations by the groups linked to the environmentalists about its over-close links with the roads lobby. John Tyme, the most passionate of the anti-road campaigners alleged that

> . . . this country does not have a Department of Transport but a
> Department of Highways, which possesses the power to make policy
> decisions on railways and waterways and, furthermore, which exercises
> this power not in the national interest, but in the interest of one
> industrial/financial lobby – in short, that it thereby constitutes a
> corruption of government and thus a major threat to our democracy.
> (1978: 92.)

More sober critics, such as Stephen Plowden and Peter Levin, have instanced the resistance of the Department of Transport to new ideas about the best way to cope with the explosion in motorized transport. They both draw attention to the domination of the road engineers within the department and the failure to bring them under any overall policy control (Plowden 1980 and Levin 1979).

Several questions need to be further examined: whether the road engineers were allowed to become too powerful within the department in relation to other sections and to dominate transport policy; whether they were too closely linked to, or influenced by, the sectional roadbuilding interests; and whether the department's officials were resistant to other viewpoints in a partisan and inequitable manner. In the context of the consensus on the need for a big road-building programme in the 1960s, there were strong pressures to get ahead with individual proposals and to shorten the time span and eliminate the delays accompanying such complicated and large-scale construction schemes. The status of the road engineers in the department was therefore enhanced and a Director-General of Highways (an engineer) was appointed to head a separate highways division in 1965. It set up six regional Road Construction Units (RCUs) to supervise the roadbuilding programme (Painter 1980b). The RCUs became powerful units in their own right, providing traffic forecasts and other justifications for their own plans. In short, there was an amalgamation of both policymaking and executive responsibility for highways in the same division within the ministry. When the ministry was amalgamated into the big conglomerate Department of the Environment in 1970, the Highways section managed to keep its independent status. From 1970–72 its director-general was at deputy secretary level, on a par with Wilfrid Burns who headed the planning section dealing with all land use and development plans, and the head of the transport industries section – the railways, ports, etc. (Draper 1977). Highways planning also stayed outside the regional policy and planning within the department (except in the South-East), because it was argued that the division had direct executive responsibilities for its programmes. By 1973 responsibility at ministerial level rejoined roads to the transport industries and further separated roads from land use and environmental planning. The status and strength of the engineers and the highways section within the department thus stayed very strong over a long period. The position of the engineers as professional specialists may be contrasted with other groups like the economists, statisticians and mathematicians within the department. They were all intermingled within the big new directorates of the Department of the Environment in the 1970s as advisers, although there was also one central Economics and Resources Division. The difference clearly lay in the fact that the engineers were running a very large, expensive and long-term roads programme. They were allowed to assume control of it in virtual independence of the rest of the department up to 1976.

The charge of excessive influence by sectional interests should also be examined. Consultation with trade interests is a normal feature of department life. That links exist and are carefully fostered is not remarkable. The BRF's job is to foster them, and the trade associations have regular contacts. Monthly visits and lunches with Department of Transport officials, for example, are said to take place by officials of the FTA and the RHA, and the RHA is asked which of the department's road schemes it particularly wants to see pushed forward (Wardroper 1981). The roads interest was said by Barbara Castle to be 'the most vociferous lobby in this country' in the 1960s.[1] Its influence was no doubt enhanced by the strong community of interest with the road engineers within the department: the trade interests wanted the contracts and the engineers wanted to build the roads for which there appeared to be strong public support. It was not so much a question of excessive influence as of total identification of the department with its clients or pressure groups. This phenomenon of 'clientelism' has been remarked as a feature of modern bureaucracies (Richardson and Jordan 1979). Sharing common priorities, the trade interests which depend on public contracts and the department which uses its programmes in the fight for resources and influence within Whitehall, join together to assist each other. The roads lobby and the highways section of the ministry in the 1960s and early 1970s provide a strong example of this phenomenon.

During this period there was insufficient counter balance to the roads interest. The highways section, as has been noted, kept its strong position within the department. The environmental movement was developing as a force but was neither as coherent nor well organized as the roads lobby. Transport 2000, for example, was run by part-time enthusiasts with the aid of a paid clerical worker up to 1977 and although it always had access to ministers because of union leadership, there was no regular contact with department officials. The LATA was not on the department's consultation list until 1976 when it was put on it by the new minister, Bill Rodgers. The conservation groups had a wide range of interests of which transport was only one. Moreover, the convictions of some officials in both central and local government were sometimes so strong that they actively sought to promote one side of the argument. For example, when LATA in 1969 came out against the policy of motorway building, 'From that moment . . . public participation by the GLC was replaced by hostility. It is now known that a chief officer of the GLC provided the British Road Federation with a detailed attack on the LATA Report for the BRF to publish. The LATA professionals became persona non grata at the Ministry of Transport and the GLC' (Thomson 1977).

Another illustration of extreme advocacy and political manoeuvring by department officials is provided by the notorious 'Peeler Memorandum' of 1976 from the then head of the Freight Directorate, Joseph Peeler, to his deputy secretary which saw the light of day through a 'leak' which led to its publication. It outlines the question of whether a committee of inquiry into lorry weights should be set up and establishes that 'For the purpose of this note it is assumed that we wish to stick to our current maximum of 10 tonnes axle weight (or its equivalent), but to move, as soon as parliamentary and public opinion will let us, to a maximum gross weight of 38 or 40 tonnes.' It then briskly proceeds to analyse the political uses to which an inquiry could be put, and how it could serve to give advantage to the road haulage interest.

> In this context the main advantage of some kind of inquiry, held wholly or partly in public, would be presentational. The case for permitting heavier lorries, and the case against put by environmental protection groups, would be aired in public and be subjected to rigorous scrutiny and questioning, if not cross examination. At the end of the day, recommendations would be made by impartial people of repute who have carefully weighed and sifted the evidence and have come to, one hopes, a sensible conclusion in line with the Department's view. Backed by such a recommendation, the government of the day will be in a stronger position to take action. The inquiry would not obviate the need for the statutory procedures, including consultation with interested parties, before the introduction of the necessary statutory instrument. But the passage through these processes should be substantially shorter and easier if preceded by a successful inquiry . . .
>
> Although the establishment in the public mind of a clear and overwhelming case on balance for heavier lorry weights is seen as the main end of the inquiry, it could well have wider effects. It should provide a focus for the various road haulage interests to get together, marshal their forces, and act cohesively to produce a really good case which should not merely establish the main point at issue but should do good to their now sadly tarnished public image. This would make it easier for the governnment to propose legislation (on lorry weights and other matters) in their favour. Ultimately such action on a combined basis could have wider consequences in other spheres, e.g. in producing far more unity and efficiency in dealing with pay matters. Again, of course, this all depends on whether the road haulage industry are equal to their opportunities.
>
> An inquiry offers a way of dealing with the political opposition to a more rational position on lorry weights; and an opportunity to the road haulage industry to improve both its public image and its organization cohesiveness. It is therefore to be welcomed.[2]

But the heyday of the motor lobby and the roadbuilders was

coming to an end. Public opposition expressed through demonstrations at motorway inquiries was backed by a growing volume of criticism of large-scale roadbuilding programmes and an intellectual attack on the premises on which it was based. The consensus was broken and the new, more cautious policy approach was outlined in the 1976 Consultation Document and 1977 White Paper. The Department of Transport was re-established in 1976 but the Highways Division lost its separate status and was placed within a Roads and Local Transport Division. A Policy Review Unit, jointly headed by an economist and an administrator, was set up to look at all future transport plans. The RCUs were reviewed and plans to phase them out (although as part of the privatization programme) were made in 1981. Environmental groups were accorded recognition and more regular consultation. And the over-confident Mr Peeler was exiled to a not too uncomfortable Siberia as director of the South East Regional Office of the department.

The motorways programme has been drastically reduced in order to cut down public expenditure and the influence of the lobby has thus suffered. The focus in 1982 has been on the burning question of lorry weights and whether they should be raised. Trade interests have backed the proposals, environmental groups resisted them and the roads lobby have used them as a justification for proposals to build by-passes to country towns. In the 1980s, Treasury restrictions on expenditure provide a stronger counter pressure on the roads and lorries lobby than was possible ten years previously and it will remain to be seen whether that influence can be reasserted against the environmental groups once economic conditions improve.

PRESSURE GROUPS, POLITICIANS, 'PARTICIPATION' AND THE PUBLIC

The organization of pressure groups, whether sectional or promotional, is designed to influence and lobby government at the levels of government or local council department, Members of Parliament or local councillors, and to influence public opinion. Pressure groups require continuous and substantial funding to operate effectively and such resources are clearly not open to individuals, or to many small societies. The desire to include as many members of the public as possible in the planning process led to the Skeffington Committee Report of 1969 which drew up proposals for participation – 'the act of sharing in the formulation of policies and proposals'. New frameworks have since been carefully devised. County councils since 1968 must publish their proposals for structure plans identifying broad policies for land use, transport and traffic management. Topics are then selected for an 'Examination in Public' when all kinds of organizations, ranging from statutory bodies and other local authorities to voluntary organizations and local societies can put forward their views for consideration. Responses are also invited to Reports of Survey and to alternative proposals. These procedures do not pre-empt later individual objections to particular details of the plans once agreed by the minister, but are intended as a broad discussion of the policy issues at county council level. The Skeffington ideal was to promote 'partnership' in the planning process between local authorities and the public, with the implication that if government and members of the public, many with opposing interests, met to discuss issues, difficulties would be resolved and a consensus achieved. The reality has not been quite so rosy; conflicts of interest inevitably remain, and it has been concluded that the participation procedures have been useful in identifying areas of conflict which have then to be resolved by 'distributional bargaining' as decisions are taken, rather than as a method of achieving consensus (Bruton 1980). But it can be said that the participation process helps to defuse the concern and feelings of helplessness which may be felt in the face of bureaucratic decisions by providing prior information and offering procedural opportunities for the discussion of policy and broad planning proposals before decisions are taken at county level.

Proposals for trunk roads and motorways and for airports are made by central government departments and parallel opportunities do not exist for discussion. The procedures used for the hearing of objections are the same as those for detailed objections to local authority plans, i.e. they are concerned with the people and property directly affected by the proposals. There was, and is, no possibility of the public debating the general policy behind the proposals at the inquiries. The problem for local people has been that the first they usually knew of a new road proposal was a report in the paper or a notice of an inquiry to be held. Fear and concern quickly escalated as they were told at the inquiries that the decisions to build the roads had been taken and could not be reviewed and that discussions on the needs and the merits of the case could only be held in Parliament, and objectors should restrict themselves to individual problems. Moreover, the determination of the government officials to speed up and achieve their targets of road construction put pressure on the timetable of which the inquiry was one aspect. As long as the desirability of the motorway programme was widely accepted there was no real difficulty. In 1962 it was possible for the Parliamentary Secretary to the Ministry of Transport to answer a fellow MP in the House of Commons speaking up for his local rural district council who were objecting to a proposed section of the M4 in the following indignant terms

> I must warn my Hon. Friend . . . that I would not be surprised if many motorists, the RAC and the AA and many others in the Bristol area had something to say to the Warmley Rural District Council for slowing up this matter . . . We shall give the Warmley Council and the residents of Warmley every opportunity to put their case, but it is our clear intention that we want to get the motorway built . . . the risk is that we will now be seriously delayed in carrying through this important and expensive scheme because one rural district council, covering a couple of miles, feels that, having agreed all the way through since 1951, it must now change its tune and have a public inquiry.[3]

The new road was clearly all-important and Warmley's (belated) objection a terrible nuisance, to be brushed aside and overcome. Over the next ten years, however, there was a change in the seeming consensus that motorways were desirable and by the 1970s a veritable eruption of anger occurred. Demonstrations at one public inquiry after another escalated to the stage of disruption with the objectors trying to raise basic disagreement and the beleagured inspectors desperately trying to hold to the official position on the permissible scope of the inquiry and indeed to maintain any kind of order.

At the Aire Valley Inquiry in Yorkshire in 1975, the police were called on the first day, the inquiry was adjourned early on the next and on the third it was adjourned for two weeks. On the day that it resumed the pandemonium was such that the police made twelve arrests. Finally 'At 11.50 Mr. Ridge (the Inspector) called on Mr. Keene for the Department of the Environment to open his case. As he rose a renewed storm of booing, shouting and clapping started. Protesters then sang the National Anthem again and then "Land of Hope and Glory"!'[4] But it was no good; two days later the inquiry was again adjourned for two months. When it restarted and an attempt was made to restrict the numbers attending, that failed, and again it was adjourned.

This pattern was repeated in different parts of the country. In Winchester in 1976 'More than 800 objectors crowded into

Winchester Guildhall today for the opening of the M 3 inquiry and shouted, chanted, stamped and clapped their way through the first half hour of the hearing . . . The Ministry Inspector . . . was continually shouted down.'[5] And the next day 'Hundreds of M 3 inquiry objectors at Winchester today chanted "Sieg Heil" 'and gave the Nazi salute as police forcibly ejected TV camera crews from the hall.' (The scenes of disorder were not to be allowed to be filmed.) When the local MP, Rear Admiral Morgan Giles, attempted to persuade the objectors that the inquiry should be used for its intended purpose – 'the conduct of the majority of the audience yesterday and today is bringing what ought to be a perfectly serious inquiry into disrepute' – he was jeered at. He shouted back the impeccable but unhelpful view that 'Democracy breaks down when organised groups break up properly constituted meetings'.[7]

In 1977 the inspector at the Highgate Archway Road inquiry was reduced to trying to hold his inquiry in a small back room (nicknamed by objectors his 'bunker') to avoid the public in the large hall for whose benefit the inquiry was ostensibly held. But that was no use either; the objectors broke in, there was a scuffle, and once more the inquiry was adjourned.

What was apparent at these inquiries to all except the department officials was that the official procedures were no longer suitable for the challenge that the objectors wanted to make. They were intended for individual objections, but the objectors wanted to hold basic policy discussions on the need for the roads, because there was nowhere else that they could do so. The fact that in some instances the basic line had been settled at earlier inquiries several years ago without comparable resistance and the new inquiries were meant (e.g. at Winchester and Archway Road) to deal only with the slip roads, was put by the inspectors but only infuriated the objectors more. Somewhere in the 1970s the consensus had broken down. The objectors began to organize themselves at the hearings. At first they had tried to seek information on which the proposals were based and to challenge the arguments, but were denied information and sometimes the necessary sight of papers. This in itself was a basic cause for grievance: information is a vital tool in any struggle and for middle class and professional people especially, unaccustomed to refusal, it was a crucial matter. During the Aire Valley inquiry, for example, a Baildon Green objector said the public had been treated like criminals by the Road Construction Unit when they tried to get information out of them. "If you want this inquiry to go into the records as an impartial one there must be none of the atmosphere of secrecy that has been going on until this moment" he said.'[8]

Spontaneously the inquiries had become political happenings where a challenge to authority was made, because there appeared to be no alternative. The Vice-Chairman of the M3 Action Group, a professor of sociology no less, observed of the Winchester affair 'People who only a few years ago were horrified by student sit-ins are now prepared to be removed forcibly from public inquiries. Indeed, they are prepared to go much farther along the paths of direct action than anyone had believed.' And 'the objectors . . . were proud to think of themselves as the political heirs of those seventeenth century squires and yeomen who were outraged by the misgovernment of the Stuarts and their reliance on non-parliamentary procedures that violated natural justice and constitutional liberties'. (Morris 1976.)

As so often, the occasion produced the man. John Tyme, a hitherto unknown lecturer in environmental studies, began to move from one inquiry to the next to rally the groups of objectors, advise them on tactics and lead the opposition. Tyme believed passionately that 'the motorway/trunk road programme with all its ramifications poses a consummate evil, and constitutes the greatest threat to the interests of this nation in all its history. None of our national enemies have so mutilated our cities, undermined our long-term economic movement of people and goods, destroyed our industrial base, diminished our ability to plan our community life, and reduced our capacity to feed ourselves.' (Tyme 1978: p. 1) He also believed that the roads lobby had hopelessly corrupted both the Department of Transport and the MPs and councillors, but still had confidence that the use of peaceful methods of 'dissent' could achieve justice for the community. John Tyme's tactics were many, but in essence he refused to observe the ministry's rules of procedure and tried to introduce his own. Usually he attempted at the start of an inquiry to introduce basic objections to the roads programme and when overruled, or not allowed to speak, uproar could usually be relied on to break out. For a short period he was a true folk hero, was awarded a three-year grant by the Rowntree Trust to pursue his work, and wrote a book setting out his views. Then quite suddenly he disappeared from public view.

But by now the government had had enough. It set up a review of highway inquiry procedures to try and repair the damage caused by the breach in public confidence in the system. The Report (Cmnd 7113) went some way to meet the grievances of objectors.

It recommended that the department's brief should be made available to objectors, and that the department should be ready to consider and report on alternative road routes and to explain the 'appropriateness' of its technical assessment methods. There would also be a procedural meeting before an inquiry started to sort out arrangements and a co-ordinator appointed to assist objectors and to provide them with facilities for examining and copying documents. On the main point, however, the report and the government stayed firm: there was to be no discussion at inquiries of the national roads policy which was the prerogative of Parliament. Annual White Papers on Roads Policy were in future to be issued which would enable Parliament to discuss not only general policy but also the major roads proposed; the first appeared in 1980.

In the last few years, the tension has lessened. The roads programme has been scaled down as public expenditure has been cut back. A change of government has reinforced the view on transport policy which links new roads to economic recovery. The relative calm does not, however, disguise the fact that the old consensus has not yet been replaced. L. J. Sharpe (1975b) points out that for 'participation' to work, there needs to be an 'operating ideology' backed by majority opinion. In the case of transport, what looked like a consensus for roadbuilding very abruptly broke down. Because of the determination of the ministry's road engineers, the failure of Parliament to act as a forum for discussion of policy and the narrowness of the inquiry procedures, there was a series of confrontations out of character for the people involved.

It is not yet clear whether a new operating ideology will emerge and what form it will take. The problems thrown up may not be capable of ready solution. Even if people are ready to accept new roadbuilding, there will always be objection when it affects immediate individual interests. A gain in national car mobility is not easily matched against an individual loss of peace and quiet. We are back to the question of the distribution of public goods: who gains and who loses? Because people's immediate and most direct position is the one about which they feel (and campaign) most strongly, the opposition to new proposals will continue to be strenuously pursued by the people adversely affected. The resolution of the issue is then likely to depend on the strength of the participants' bargaining position, in terms of their resources, and ability to organize and to enlist politicians' support; in other words to an essentially political process of struggle.

In such a competition for favourable decisions and public goods, some groups may be expected to win more readily than others. In one study of local groups in four London boroughs which had effected changes in council policy, it was noted that professional resources and skills and independent financial resources were important (Chamberlayne 1978). Another analysis also mentions resources, together with the ability to get hold of advance intelligence, to liaise with administrators and legislators and to present a rational argument (Kimber and Richardson 1974a). A leading participant of the M3 Action Group noted that it was 'one of the most articulate and best organised groups in the country. As well as being able to raise more money than most, it could call on the professional skills of its own member architects, engineers, lawyers, computer experts and public relations men' (Morris 1976). The strong professional input which LATA was able to contribute to the evidence to the Greater London Development Plan Inquiry and its analysis of the issues was undoubtedly a contributory factor to its success. But if professional expertise and financial resources are crucial factors, it is very likely that the 'sharp elbows of the middle classes' will once again secure the greatest benefits. Indeed, some of the criticism of participation in planning is that it benefits only the elite groups who are articulate and well organized (Bruton 1980) and some, like Tony Crosland, discounted the environment movement as a middle-class exercise (Crosland 1974).

How far is this accusation of middle-class elitism true? Certainly the range of organizations involved in the procedures of participation allied to county structure plans is likely to be limited to the established and organized groups within the community. In Bedfordshire, for example, the organizations responding to the county council's *Report of Surveys and Alternatives* were the local amenity societies, community and church organizations, representative employer and labour groups and local political parties. At the Examination in Public, the response to the transport proposals was made by British Rail, the National Bus Company, the AA, the Cyclists' Touring Club and the Midlands Motorway Action Group (Blowers 1980). We also know that participation in local government and voluntary activity is closely linked to the extent of peoples' full-time education. The Royal Commission on Local Government of 1969 found this correlation. A study of the characteristics of the M3 motorway group activists found that thirty-three out of the thirty-nine involved had had higher education (Dowse and Hughes 1977). As education beyond school leaving age continues to expand to benefit more people, there should be a wider spread of the propensity to participate. But if professional skills are crucial and cannot be provided from community resources, working-class communities will suffer in the planning process. However, other strengths continue to be important. The objectors at inquiries in the 1970s after all made their point by protest and obstruction, which require determination and solidarity rather than professional expertise. These qualities are universal and are, for example, important in trade union action. And in the extraordinary circumstances of Belfast, it was observed that an urban motorway planned for the city was stopped short when the official IRA and the UDA both threatened direct action against any attempt to build it (Wiener 1976). Political influence can result from the exercise of negative power too. Educational levels, professional skills and the ability to organize politically should therefore be separated. For continuing pressure group work, the first is likely to be important and for effective input into established inquiry and consultation procedures, the first and second. But for effective protest action, neither matters as much as political muscle and the will to resist.

The battles over motorway and airport proposals originated very much from the grass roots; the lead was not taken by politicians who were often responsible for the proposals. As the struggles developed, more MPs and local councillors associated themselves with the protest groups and spoke up for their constituents' views. At particular stages in the struggles, e.g. the rejection in 1967 of the proposals for the Stansted Airport, their action was crucial (Jay 1980).

In another major struggle over transport policy, more conventional political combat has taken place. The conflict over the question of subsidies for public transport has been one between the political parties and between two levels of government. The possibility of the conflict was rooted in the 1968 Transport Act which gave local authorities powers to subsidize passenger transport operations on the one hand, and the 1973 Department of the Environment circular which required local authorities to submit their transport policies or programmes for approval by central government as a basis for the TSG on the other. At political level, it can be seen in the preference of the Conservatives for open competition between transport modes and for private as opposed to public enterprise, and of Labour for 'co-ordination' in transport and for sustaining public transport services.

Proposals for extensive subsidies to public transport clearly originated at local party level in the Labour Party. For example, in

South Yorkshire in 1973 the Labour Group on Sheffield Council set out its aim that 'public transport should be regarded both as a social service and as an instrument of planning policy'. It would provide free public transport for the elderly and handicapped immediately and 'this will be regarded as a first step towards the ultimate provision of free public transport for all' (Blunkett 1982). In 1972, a resolution was passed by the Greater London Regional Council of the Labour Party setting out the aim of free public transport. This resolution found its way into Labour's 1973 GLC manifesto as a pledge to postpone further fare increases, and to start consultations for the introduction of a low flat fare system 'leading to a free transport system which is our long-term aim'. Both councils set out to carry out these policies in the face of considerable coolness on the part of Labour government ministers. Fares were frozen and restructured fare systems considered. But central government had never intended that local authorities should have an open-ended call on tax resources to finance the subsidies. The Department of the Environment saw its role in deciding the grant allocations as helping local authorities to decide on their priorities which should accord with national transport objectives and get good value for money. It foresaw for itself 'a fairly strong method of influence over the way in which they tackled their transport problems'.[9] Moreover in 1975 'In current circumstances, the need to encourage transport plans which are economical in their demands on resources now looms larger than the original wish to encourage higher transport expenditure in particular cases.'[10] In both South Yorkshire and London, the department therefore said it would penalize the councils by withdrawal of grant if the amount proposed for subsidy in the TPPs continued to rise. South Yorkshire Council stuck to its low fares policy but the pressure caused the GLC in 1976 to yield and rises in fares were approved. Instead the GLC transport chairman convened a campaigning group consisting of trade unions, public transport user associations and other civic, women's, youth and residents' groups to 'Save our Public Transport Services', and to support the council's motion pressing the government to help the council to give the necessary financial support (Greater London Council *Minutes* 1977(a)). After a three-year period in opposition from 1977 to 1981, the 1981 Labour GLC election campaign was fought on a promise to reduce fares immediately by 25 per cent and after the election victory plans to implement the policy were immediately put into effect. When the Conservative government retaliated by withdrawing grant, the

GLC proceeded to levy a supplementary rate to meet the deficit and this precipitated the challenge in the courts by Bromley Council.

Once the House of Lords' decision had gone against the GLC, political opposition was mobilized. The GLC itself began a 'Keep Fares Fair' campaign with meetings all over London. Douglas Jay MP introduced a Bill in the House of Commons to change the law relating to the subsidy. The local political party campaign was matched by other groups. The transport trade unions in London set up a London Transport Trade Union defence committee run from the TGWU headquarters. A series of some twenty local campaign groups sprang up and came together into a 'Fares Fight' campaign, often loosely linked to local Labour parties and trades councils. Other groups tried a (short-lived) 'Can't Pay Won't Pay' campaign to refuse to pay the higher fares required. Elsewhere in the country, councils were urgently querying the legality of their own subsidies and the West Midlands Council decided to comply with the supposed threat. But South Yorkshire Council decided to hold on and the South Yorkshire County Labour Party launched a political campaign to try to influence national government policy. It organized a petition which received 300,000 signatures in a month and was duly presented in London. In South Yorkshire too, the transport trade unions were in strong support and organized a twenty-four-hour strike in Sheffield against any cuts in services (Blunkett 1982).

Unlike the opposition to new motorways and airports, the policies of subsidy to public transport were started by and sustained largely through the party political machinery. The motivation was on the one hand the desire to promote effective local public transport systems and on the other to benefit the least well-off in the community who were the most dependent on them. Subsidy also represents a visible benefit which politicians can promise to the electorate and, like rents, once fares are frozen it is not easy for them to be raised. Governments of both political complexions prompted by the Treasury fears about open-ended subsidies, tried hard from the beginning to prevent local authorities from going down this particular road. The Lords' decision on the GLC case and subsequent 100 per cent fares rise has given a severe jolt to all the parties involved. The popularity of the low fares prompted a spontaneous organization of protest groups which have since backed the Labour councils and parties campaigning. But it is by no means clear how low fares have rated in popularity against the high rate levels which, without central government support, have accompanied them.

While local Labour politicians led the campaigns for public transport subsidies, they were much slower to perceive the issues of environment raised spontaneously by local residents' groups. The reason lies in the perceived relevance of environment to localities; local labour parties and trade unions were as likely to see airports and roads as links to economic prosperity and employment as intrusions to their environment. Moreover, there was in the 1960s and 1970s already a tremendous upheaval in progress in the replanning and rebuilding of towns of which road proposals only formed one part. But where roads were seen as destructive of communities, working-class areas did mobilize opposition. It was after all at Westway in London that the first major demonstrations were held in 1970 against a motorway with banners proclaiming 'Let us out of this hell: rehouse us now'. Conservative politicians also faced a dilemma. Their party has strongly favoured the rights of motorists and the motorway programme. The protest groups expressed the viewpoint of those affected and the politicians had to reconcile the need to represent their constituents' views with their party's aims. On public transport subsidies the issue is clearer; like the Bromley councillors, most Conservatives represent areas with high car ownership where the heavy rate burden of subsidies is much more apparent than the benefits of cheap public transport fares.

The movement of opinion within the political parties and on the part of the public has thus been both fast and complex. Roads have been perceived both as an opportunity and an intrusion, railways and public transport as a benefit and a burden, airports as an economic future and an environmental blight. Often the movements have been contradictory and have been reflected in the shifts within the political parties. If politicians reflect the nation, their inconsistencies mirror the dynamism of the transport scene and the public's varying reactions to it.

NOTES

1. Castle, Barbara, 4.7.1973 in the House of Commons, in Hamer (1974) p. 1.
2. A reproduction of the letter and proposed inquiry into heavier lorries from Mr Joseph Peeler to Mr Peter Lazarus as released to Transport 2000.

3. House of Commons debate March 1962, quoted by R. Gregory (1974) p. 112.
4. *Telegraph and Argus* 18.11.1975. Bradford.
5. *Southern Evening Echo* 29.6.1976. Southampton.
6. Ibid. 30.6.1976.
7. Ibid. 30.6.1976.
8. *Telegraph and Argus* 4.11.1975. Bradford.
9. Layfield Report, App. I, para. 9.
10. Ibid., para. 14.

Chapter seven

POLICY ISSUES

Policy issues for transport in the 1980s have quickly emerged. Some are a continuation of the debates of the 1970s concerning the relationship of transport to the environment and the place of traffic restraint in the cities. Others, in the harsher economic climate, question not the desirable, but the minimum needs for capital investment in transport, whether for new roads, rail equipment or airports, and link them to employment and the generation of jobs. The question of the appropriateness of subsidies to passenger transport is a debate of increased weight and urgency. The problems for people living in rural areas have multiplied as trains and bus services have been withdrawn and their difficulty in gaining access to basic services has greatly increased.

THE BATTLE FOR THE ENVIRONMENT

The great battles of the 1960s and 1970s were fought over proposals to build new roads and airports, and to limit the use of heavy lorries. Many victories were achieved by the resistance organizations, composed of local residents' groups, civic and conservation societies. Their viewpoint was recognized in the conclusion of the 1976 DOE Transport Policy Consultation Document that 'Central and local government must therefore set themselves a clear environmental objective when taking transport decisions'.

Roadbuilding

The first and almost archetypal struggle was over the proposal for an Oxford inner relief road. The Christchurch Meadows road proposal first appeared in Dr Thomas Sharp's report for Oxford City Council in 1945. It was intended to relieve the problem of traffic congestion in the High Street and the central shopping area and to safeguard the unique townscape of Oxford by providing a by-pass for through traffic across 'the miasma-bound unused meadow'.[1] When the Oxford City Council adopted the proposal in 1955, controversy immediately began. Because the town was Oxford, the college most affected was Christchurch, and five current Cabinet ministers, including the prime minister Anthony Eden, were former Christchurch men, the debate leapt into national prominence. Furious letters in *The Times*, intense lobbying and a discussion reported in the Cabinet itself, made it almost a national pastime to follow developments in the row. The many events included the canvassing of alternative routes which would affect the colleges less, but it was not until 1972 that the proposal was effectively killed after a newly elected Labour majority on the council withdrew it (Newman 1980).

In spite of the special flavour of the Oxford dispute, it included what were typical features of the roads v. environment confrontation. The first was the development of three phases of thought concerning traffic congestion in cities; a general acceptance in the 1950s of roadbuilding as a solution without traffic restraint; a reliance in the 1960s on the Buchanan formula of a new road for through traffic combined with traffic restraint and traffic-free precincts; and a move in the 1970s against all new roadbuilding and a policy instead of car restraint and priority for public transport. The second was a move in influence within local authority administration away from the engineers and towards the planners. Whereas the plans for the phases of the 1950s and 1960s were prepared by the engineers' departments, the planning departments took over the third-phase plans of the 1970s. The third was the development of active, effective campaigning against the proposals by groups of the residents affected. Although opinion within the university, between town groups and often within the city council across party lines was divided, the singleminded persistence of Christchurch College's campaign eventually achieved its objective. Of that campaign it has been said (Newman 1980):

> From one point of view it can be seen as a rich and powerful but numerically small group, exerting, openly or deviously, a degree of influence which could be called the antithesis of democracy . . . From another viewpoint, Christchurch can be seen as an early example of the effectiveness of local protest . . . there can be little doubt that their system of protest was effective long enough, until the changes in public opinion in the last decade were sufficient to catch up . . . and Oxford was

therefore saved from the construction of a road system through its centre, which by current opinion would be abhorrent.

The last typical feature was the conversion of a local political party to the environment case. In Oxford, it was the change of view of the City Labour Party, which subsequently won control of the local council, which ended the road proposal. But political party opinion was not initially supportive; it took the canvassing of the protest groups and a change in the climate of thought to bring it about.

The larger-scale battle over the London ringway roads followed similar lines, although the process was vastly more expensive. The ringway proposals had their origins in Sir Patrick Abercrombie's Greater London Plan of 1945, which proposed five ringways to link the radial routes and to act as concentric rings round London's development. In modified version, Abercrombie's proposals were written into the LCC's Development Plans. Then the London Traffic Survey of 1964 and London Transportation Study of 1966 studied traffic movement and the projected increase in car ownership and these formed the bases of the road proposals of the Greater London Development Plan of 1969. Three ringways were to be built of dual- three- or four-lane capacity (i.e. six or eight lanes in all). In innocence of the coming public reaction, the Greater London Development Plan Statement (para. 5.21) put the view that: 'Ringway One provides an opportunity to improve an unsatisfactory environment. Much of its route lies through obsolete areas which urgently need rebuilding'. When the loss of housing and the impact of the roads became apparent, opposition quickly built up. The borough councils on the route of the ringway voiced their opposition. Local residents' groups and civic societies joined together to form the LMAG. A 'Homes before Roads' Party was formed to contest the GLC elections of 1970 and received 71,000 votes. Meanwhile, the cost estimates of the ringways escalated to £2,000 m. in 1972. The government's decision in 1970 to hold a full-scale inquiry into the Greater London Development Plan by a panel headed by Sir Frank Layfield, QC introduced a new element of public participation which gave the opposition groups opportunity to present their own evidence. Seventy-five percent of all the objections made to the Greater London Development Plan were to transport proposals and it took the panel sixty-three days to hear evidence on strategic transport proposals and a further sixty-seven days for the objections to local transport issues. Protesting groups were able to put forward objections to the data and forecasting techniques on which the proposals were based, to point to the failure to consider alternatives, and to emphasize the cost of the roads as well as their environmental impact. The struggle also took place to convert the London Regional Council of the Labour Party. Labour's endorsement of the ringways in 1967 gave way to uneasiness and opposition to Ringway One in 1970 and eventually to direct opposition at the 1973 elections. By 1973 the Layfield Panel's recommendation in favour of Ringway One only, to siphon-off heavy traffic and 'make possible the environmental improvements in the Central Area which are so badly needed' was a lame duck (Dept of Environment 1973a: para. 12.64). The newly elected Labour controlled GLC of 1973 withdrew the ringway proposals from the development plan.

The London ringways controversy included the same features as the Oxford inner relief road: reliance on roadbuilding, aimed first to improve traffic congestion, then to 'protect' environment; a shift from the road engineers' to the planners' perspective; following a shift in view of the party which gained majority control (Labour); resulting from the vigorous campaign of grass roots organizations.

A similar process of change is also described in a study of road proposals in the three cities of Portmouth, Southampton and Nottingham over the same period, although in Portsmouth the political change came through new councillors of the majority party and not through a change in party control (Grant 1977).

In the 1970s, resistance to individual national motorway proposals reached new heights, with the development of methods of objection hitherto unseen at the previously sedate planning inquiries. The inquiries were intended to deal with the objection of local people to proposals which directly affected them. The objectors wanted to use them to object to the need for the roads at all. The result in some cases was a series of confrontations which saw procedural objections escalate to speeches from the floor, obstruction, the calling in of the police and the indefinite adjournment of the inquiries. It became evident that normal 'inquiry' procedures could not be used where the underlying consensus of views was missing. Clearly the consensus for major roadbuilding was gone by the 1970s and the environmental case could not easily be overriden. Expenditure on new motorways was then steadily scaled down.

Airport building

A parallel struggle over the building of a third London Airport has taken place since the 1950s. Many of the same features have been present. Proposals have been put forward by civil aviation experts, based on air traffic forecasts and projections, which have been rejected by land use planners and by local councils and residents' groups. An attempt was made to solve the conflicts about a choice of site through 'rational' planning and the use of cost benefit analysis by the Roskill Commission of Inquiry. Its report of 1970 and recommendation for Cublington was overthrown under the pressure of the environmentalists in favour of the minority report of Colin Buchanan recommending the coastal site of Maplin. Maplin in its turn was discarded after a change of government in 1974 as too costly and falsely prestigious. For the first time a national airports strategy was considered. The White Paper *Airport Policy* (Dept of Trade 1978) included both consumer demand and the environmental and land use implications of aircraft developments among its basic assumptions, and stressed the need for flexible planning and development related to demand growth and a recognition of the employment and economic development prompted by airports. It forecast the need for a significant increase in capacity at the London area airports from 31 m. passengers in 1976 to between 66 m. and 89 m. in 1990. It concluded that the development of existing airports should be limited, with Heathrow and Gatwick each adding one further terminal, and Stansted increasing its capacity from 300,000 passengers in 1976 up to 4 m. by the 1990s, with its one runway and an extension of its existing terminal. It did note, however, that Stansted, surrounded by a largely rural area and thus with the least adverse noise effects on the scattered population, was in line as an option for long-term development. That option was taken up by the government in 1981 with a proposal for expansion of capacity to 15 m., a new terminal and the safeguarding of land for a second runway.

The revival of the Stansted option owes much to the quiet persistence of the civil aviation lobby and its supporters in the government departments. The political stances of the parties have been less clear: while Conservatives in the country areas affected have espoused the environmental cause, Conservative governments have adopted the viewpoint favouring economic benefits, as indeed did the Labour minister, Tony Crosland, in the 1970s. The querying of the need for a new airport has only recently developed.

The 1979 Report of the Advisory Committee on Airports Policy argues that the case for a larger airport at Stansted rests on expanding tourist needs (foreign leisure passenger traffic was projected by the 1978 White Paper to double for London airports between

1975–85 and to triple between 1975–90); the needs of the British air transport industry (the UK airlines carry more international passengers than any others); the promotion of business and trade; and the creation of large numbers of new jobs. Colin Buchanan, championing the cause of rural Essex and Hertfordshire, asserts that the forced 'urbanization' of some 200 square miles of largely open countryside, combined with a direct loss of about 20,000 acres of good agricultural land, contravenes land use policy and environmental considerations. He puts the case against expanded tourism and an open-ended policy of meeting air traffic demand, and for making better use of the existing airports, subject to stringent environmental controls. Drawing a deliberate parallel with the assumptions behind roads policy in the 1950s and 1960s Buchanan concludes (1980: 113–14):

> The industry would no doubt claim that the approach I have outlined, namely to make the best use of the airport system we already have, would be tantamount to saying that there is a limit to the amount of airport capacity that can be provided in this country. That might well be the case, but what of it? Who says that air travel is such an overwhelming good that it must be accommodated regardless of all other considerations? There is a precedent. Until fairly recently, motor car travel was regarded as an overwhelming good to be accommodated to the full extent of demand. But not now. The tide has turned. No authority now plans to accommodate all the demands that may arise; in the cities especially, the emphasis is increasingly turning to restrictive policies. What has caused the swing? Shortage of funds to some extent, but overwhelmingly it is the result of environmental concern. Would it be disaster irremediable if the same thing were to happen to air transport? I doubt it. Air travel, after all, is not everything, but the face of Britain is. The island is all we have, there is no other place to go.

The stage is clearly set for a further conflict and trial of strength between the environmentalists and those putting the case for economic benefits at both local and national level. Since the national government will have to decide, the environmentalists' aim will be to influence MPs and bring pressure to bear on government to drop the proposals. After the long trail from civil aviation's choice (Stansted), through 'rational' planning (Cublington), the environmentalists' choice (Maplin), and a more cautious limited development option (the 1978 White Paper), we are back again at a bigger expansion for Stansted. Limitations on public expenditure have prevented any future grandiose plans on the scale of Cublington or Maplin. In 1982 the policy of the 1978 White Paper was adopted as the basis for new development. The fourth terminal at Heathrow was being built and the decision was taken to build a second terminal at Gatwick. Stansted's future will be determined once the public inquiry is completed. A decision to build a new terminal, with further safeguarding of land for future use, will signify the effective erosion of the environmentalists' position, and set the stage for the further expansion of Stansted as London's third airport.

Lorries

The objections to the large 'juggernaut' lorries favoured by the road haulage industry are their size, weight, fumes, noise and vibration. The height, width and length of the large lorries is out of proportion with the human scale of people, streets and shops. They overwhelm the pedestrian visually. Their length provokes problems of manoeuvring round corners and down narrow streets which adds to the perception of menace and contributes to traffic congestion and delay. Their weight is chiefly perceived through noise and vibration as they pass by. The heavy lorry passing through residential areas or down quiet country roads is a danger and an intrusion; in shopping and commercial centres it is a traffic congestant as well. Public reaction to large lorries is a part of the dislike of traffic noise, fumes and vibration and fears about danger to pedestrians which has been found in surveys of public attitudes (Dept of Environment 1978). It is not only lorries which provoke this reaction (motor cycles are also very unpopular), but they are particularly remarked as a source of difficulty. A survey in North Yorkshire, for example, found that 78 per cent of respondents wanted heavy lorries to be restricted and 26 per cent put restriction as their first choice as a transport policy; this preference increased in importance the higher the household's socio-economic group (Courtenay 1977).

The number of very large, heavy lorries has increased dramatically in the last ten years (see Table 1.6, p. 12) and industry has consistently pressed for an increase in permitted weights from the 32.5 tonnes limit up to the 40 or 44 tonne maximum of several EEC countries. The pressure has been put not only at national level but also on the EEC where proposals to harmonize permitted lorry weights upwards to 40 tonnes have been under consideration for some years. The arguments in favour of larger heavier lorries arise from the internal logic of modern industrial and commercial developments. Freight movement has greatly increased in the past decade. More goods are carried for longer distances as a direct result of specialization within industry. Components are manufactured at factories in one part of the country and brought to another for assembly, or imported from another country. Some large national firms concentrate their products in a few big units whose products have then to be distributed all over the country; the smaller factory supplying local or regional needs is far less important than it was. The location of industry has also had important effects on transport. Sites are now increasingly in industrial estates and on the outskirts of cities which have to be serviced by lorries. Another factor is the recent development within the retail trade. Large retail supermarkets and hypermarkets allow for economies of scale, and cheaper products through bulk purchase. These units are often located outside city centres and require large-scale lorry deliveries.

The tendency to build a few national or regional depots from which stocks are delivered can be seen in both manufacturing and the retail trades. United Biscuits, for example, has 12 principal factories and distributes from 20 distribution depots, mostly through its own lorry fleet. Beechams, manufacturing food and drinks, cosmetics and medicines has 12 factories and 18 depots, and its soft drinks division (Corona) has 15 factories and 55 depots to deliver to some 80,000 customers in canteens, hotels, cafes and clubs. Sainsbury's undertake daily deliveries to their 224 retail outlets; every supermarket is likely to receive 25 deliveries a week from the firm's own depots and a further 75 from direct suppliers (Freight Transport Association 1979). Although transport costs vary in importance for different types of trade and industry – they are clearly greater for heavy bulky products than small light ones – any reduction is helpful to trade economics. The increased cost of haulage following the acceptance of the tachograph and the regulation of drivers' working hours has emphasized for both hauliers and trade interests the need for other possible cost reductions. Overall, the CBI estimated in 1981 that £500 m. per annum could be saved in industrial costs if lorry weights were increased to 44 tonnes. (Confederation of British Industry 1981).

In 1980 the Armitage Report *Lorries, People and the Environment* recommended an increase in permitted lorry weights to 44 tonnes for five axles and combined this recommendation with others designed to reduce the admitted environmental problems. Its recommendation was (as the erstwhile head of the Freight Division, J. Peeler, had hoped) in line with the long-standing wishes of the

The politics of transport

Department of Transport. The government put forward its own proposals in a White Paper (Department of Transport 1980) for an increase to only 40 tonnes, together with a package of proposals for more road by-passes, consideration of lorry routes and lorry action areas, progressive reduction of lorry noise levels and increased heavy-lorry taxation. The problem was, as ever, the consistently strong public reaction to the implementation of the proposals, voiced through MPs and local councils. The Civic Trust, which had been prominent in the earlier campaign of the 1970s, again came into action to oppose increased lorry weights together with the CPRE, Transport 2000, the local authority associations representing the urban areas (Association of Metropolitan Authorities) and the district councils (Association of District Councils) and the Royal Town Planning Institute. The TGWU also opposed the increase in permitted weights and the County Councils Association have said that they could only accept it if all the ameliorative recommendations were implemented. Opposition from backbench MPs has also been strong. In December 1981, the minister, David Howell, only asked the House of Commons to defer any decision on the proposals in the White Paper until further consultations had taken place. Even so, eleven Conservative MPs voted against the motion and in favour of a Labour amendment to reject any increase in the maximum permitted weights. It took another year before the government eventually put regulations to Parliament to raise the weight limit to 38 tonnes.

The critics of the proposals have a series of points to make, based on the proposition that 'goods vehicles should be adapted to suit the environment rather than the reverse' (Council for the Protection of Rural England 1979). One set of measures would seek to reverse the movement of freight from rail to road and to use the inland waterways, especially the tidal rivers, for more freight transport. The problems here are very much connected with industry's own movement away from the railways, largely to increase their flexibility of operations, the inadequate investment in railway freight facilities and the poor siting of railway outlets in relation to modern factories and warehouses. The last determined attempt to revive railway freight was through the 1968 Act when the NFC was set up and the freightliners network was projected with lorries feeding fifty rail terminals for long-distance rail transport. The Act also included a proposal for quantity licensing of lorries exceeding 16 tons weight for distances exceeding 100 miles once the freightliners had been established. This proposal had been strenuously opposed at the time by the department. The minister, Barbara Castle, noted the 'ill concealed hostility' to the proposed Bill and especially to the idea of an integrated transport policy: 'Quantity licensing – I might have been proposing publicly-financed sin or something'[2]; it was never implemented and was formally repealed in 1980. The freight-liners system was set up but the NFC's variable performance in the 1970s put the prospects for greater integration into doubt. A further criticism of government's discrimination against the rail-ways has been the low level of taxation of lorries. The government has accepted that road haulage has not met the costs of road con-struction and maintenance in the past and therefore the competition with rail, which has to finance its own track costs, has not been on an equal basis. The 1981 Transport Act alters the basis and amount of vehicle excise duty in a bid to remedy this situation.

If the predominance of road haulage in freight transport is rec-ognized (and it seems unlikely that transfer to rail or water could dramatically affect the present proportions) the question of remov-ing or ameliorating the environmental problems associated with the larger heavier lorries arises. 'Civilizing the lorry' has been a long-standing aim, slow to be realized. As early as 1963, the Wilson Committee on noise abatement recommended a maximum of 85 dB for lorry noise. The maximum for new lorries was set at 89 dB in 1970 but never enforced. Only in 1983 will new regulations for a maximum of 88 dB be applicable to all the heaviest lorries. The development of a new heavy lorry with a maximum noise of 80 dB is now thought possible, but is not projected until the 1990s. Other proposals for greater safety and less vibration and pollution are also on the cards and could gradually be realized.

Another set of proposals concerns the diversion of heavy lorry traffic from narrow unsuitable roads in both towns and the country-side to roads away from residential centres and able to take the heavier axle weights with less wear and tear. A programme of new road by-passes has been proposed by government (and enthusiasti-cally welcomed by the BRF), but the Civic Trust has pointed out that it will cover only 60 per cent of the towns and villages likely to be on main lorry routes, leaving 40 per cent without the protec-tion considered necessary (Civic Trust 1982). Earlier proposals in 1976 to create a national network of lorry routes along existing roads had failed because of their unsuitability and the objection of communities along the designated routes. Some lorry bans by individual local authorities have taken place under the 'Dykes' Act of 1973, the best-known of which is in Windsor. The GLC's heavy lorry inquiry is now examining the same possibility for London. The Armitage Report proposed the designation of lorry action areas where special steps could be taken to alleviate the effects of lorries, but the Department of Transport is now proposing to set limits to the number of such areas by establishing a minimum amount of lorry traffic in a locality before a lorry action area could be declared.

One proposed solution to the problem of lorries is for freight complexes or distribution centres on the outskirts of towns similar to those developed in several cities in Europe. Long-distance lorries bring goods to the centre's depots where they are broken down into smaller loads for delivery to the city by lighter vehicles. Through the offices of a 'broker', the big lorries can then pick up a load for their return journey. The complex at Garanor, outside Paris, provides for a wide range of operations including warehouses and the packing and assembly of products, as well as an agency for 'matching' lorry consignments, hostel accommodation for lorry drivers and secure lorry parking facilities. The original concept of a 'break bulk' centre has however been somewhat diluted in this diversification of activities. The Garanor complex provided the example for development studies for a transhipment depot initiated by the GLC (Greater London Council 1977(b)). A proposal to develop a site at Neasden for a freight complex still awaits the secretary of state's decision on planning permission in 1982. A similar proposal for Wakefield in Yorkshire is closer to realization.

PASSENGER TRANSPORT – THE QUESTION OF SUBSIDIES

The question whether passenger transport should be subsidized from taxation is currently one of the most controversial issues in transport policy as it affects the public. The issue has arisen because the tremendous increase in car ownership has subjected the public forms of passenger transport by rail and bus to increasing competition, with the result that they have lost commercial viability over a wide range of their services. The groups who do not own or do not have the major use of a car now suffer from a greater degree of disadvantage than previously, both relative to car owners and absolutely, because so many public transport services have been reduced. The modern passenger transport picture is one of a much enhanced mobility for a substantial group of family units, but a deteriorating position for the lower-income groups, the elderly, children and young people, women in families where the man commutes to work by car, and those living in rural areas with reduced access to all kinds of facilities.

The public transport operators have had to face a situation of declining demand. The response of cutting-back services and raising fares has accelerated their deteriorating position, since poorer services and higher prices have prompted more people into buying or using cars instead. Both rail and bus services have largely gone into the red. British Rail since the 1960s has sustained a deficit at the service levels which it operates, in spite of the cutback in lines and services following the Beeching Report. Its inter-city services are the only part of its passenger services to be financially viable and these are now challenged by private bus companies. Commuter services as well as the stopping-services, cross-country routes and rural branch lines cannot be run on a commercial basis. The National Bus Company had in 1980 moved back into profit led by its long-distance coach services after a period of losses, but its local bus services have steadily gone into the red as passenger journeys and bus mileage have declined. The railways have to finance the heavy fixed costs of track, signalling and stations from a far more limited clientele. The bus situation is slightly different; fixed costs are less important, but staff salaries for the National Bus Company, for example, are nearly 70 per cent of the total costs in spite of the extensive switch to one-man operation, and bus drivers cannot be dispensed with when buses run half-empty.

Left to themselves, local rail and bus services would largely disappear in the face of competition from private cars and only the inter-city services would continue to operate. Roads would become more congested, even as more were built to accommodate the cars, and cities would either be choked with traffic, or would be radically changed to accommodate the new roads. In the 1960s and 1970s the options were either to go for the American experience with a greater roadbuilding programme, or to reverse the trend with a combination of measures of restraint on road traffic and assistance to public transport. Although the motorway solution was widely urged and planned for in the 1960s, it ran into the opposition of fierce environmental protest which, combined with a new financial stringency in relation to public expenditure, brought a full-scale motorways solution to a halt. The alternative of subsidizing public transport services in combination with measures of traffic restraint was instead increasingly used in the 1970s in an effort to find a more balanced solution.

Subsidy from government to public transport can take various forms. The most obvious is subsidies from general taxation or the local rates to maintain services which would otherwise be cut and to reduce the level of fares which would otherwise be charged. But subsidy can also take the form of grants for capital expenditure, or granting relief from taxation which would otherwise be levied and thus reducing costs, or even the possibility of direct 'voucher' payments to consumers to enable them to buy transport services. The 1968 Transport Act used several types of subsidy. It empowered central government to make capital grants for transport operators' infrastructure, to subsidize rail services specified as socially necessary but unviable financially, and to assist running costs by a rebate on fuel duty. It also allowed local authorities to support public transport services in their areas through subsidies to the new PTAs. The 1972 Local Government Act gave the same powers to all county councils and required them to produce a 'balanced' programme of transport policies and expenditure every year (the TPPs, introduced from 1974). Public Transport Plans were also required to be submitted by the shire counties under the Transport Act, 1978.

Table 7.1 shows that total direct subsidy to passenger transport by both central and local government was £923 m. in 1975/76 (at 1980 prices) but has dropped to £789 m. in 1980/81. The single largest amount went to British Rail from central government (£454 m.) to finance the PSO set out in terms of the 1974 Railways Directive. The bulk of the local authority subsidy went to the buses. In 1979/80 £197 m. was paid for bus, Underground and ferry services, £118 m. for concessionary fares for pensioners and others, and £32 m. to British Rail.

Turning to the type of subsidy, most expenditure goes on meeting the net costs of operators' undertakings, at the service level which government, either central or local, requires. Thus the PSO payment to British Rail provides for meeting the obligation to sustain a level of service comparable to that provided in 1974. Two-thirds of local authority expenditure also falls into this category of general subsidy, but some of it is directed towards financing the operation of specific services provided by road or rail. There has recently been a strong movement on the part of the metropolitan counties to subsidize general fare levels in order to keep them from rising, and with the aim of stimulating higher public transport use. A more specific subsidy directed to reduce fares has been the concessionary fares for pensioners. Other types of grant to the National Bus Company from central government, now being phased out, have been new bus grants, infrastructure grants, rural bus service

Table 7.1   Public expenditure on inland surface transport 1975/76 –
1980/81 (£m. at 1980 survey prices)

	1975/76	1979/80	1980/81
1. Roads			
Motorways and trunk roads			
new construction and improvement	635	352	320
maintenance	93	114	102
Local roads			
new construction and improvement	540	342	*
maintenance	623	558	547
Total, all roads	1,891	1,366	
2. Payments to transport operator			
Central government:			
to British Rail – passenger subsidies	496	449	454
– other payments	349	201	112
New bus grants	37	34	34
Other	14	16	13
Local government:			
Passenger transport subsidies			
– British Rail	28	32	225
– bus, underground and ferry	288	197	
Concessionary fares subsidies	113	118	110
Public transport investment	255	188	*
Total, all payments	1,580	1,235	
3. Other expenditure			
Department of Transport			
Driver and vehicle licensing	83	51	57
Research and other services	43	12	13
Roads and transport administration	30	26	26
Other local expenditure and			
administration	215	195	*
Total expenditure	3,860	2,887	2,724

*Source: The Government's Expenditure Plans 1981–82 to 1983–84, 1981,
Cmnd 8175, HMSO*

* For 1980/81, the amount of capital expenditure by local authorities on
road construction and improvements, public transport and car parks is
aggregated to give a total of £544 m.

grants and the rebate on fuel duty. British Rail has received special
replacement allowances for equipment.

The grants mentioned are all specified in public transport operators' accounts. Other types of subsidy not included as contri-

butions to transport include the free bus services often provided by local authorities to bring the elderly and the handicapped to day centres and schools and the rural school bus services. Ambulance services provided to bring people to hospital clinics and health centres also fall within the scope of subsidized transport. None of these subsidies are quantified as such.

The objectives of subsidy are various. First and foremost they are aimed at maintaining the viability of public transport operations, by increasing the custom and the receipts of the undertakings and thus enabling them to continue to run a network of services. As part of this objective, the intention is that the subsidy will improve the efficiency of the undertaking by providing improved services. Second, viable public transport operations contribute to the achievement of several other broader aims. One is the contribution which the services make to the economy and vitality of cities and conurbations; without comprehensive and reasonably priced public transport networks, offices, shops and factories in the cities cannot be serviced with workers, and the city centre shopping and entertainments cannot find their customers. Another is the reduction in economic costs which should be realized through a reduction in traffic congestion as the number of commuter cars is reduced. Third and more far-reaching is the purpose of overall saving in energy resources achieved through the more efficient use of petrol in buses or electricity in trains. Fourth, thriving public transport also contributes to the aim of preserving a good environment by reducing motor traffic with its negative features of noise, fumes and threat to pedestrians, by pleasant and safer surroundings, and by making unnecessary the building of new roads. Fifth, there is the broad social objective of making transport available at reasonable cost to the 40 per cent of households concentrated in the lower income levels who do not have cars or to those members of the households who do not have easy access to the one car owned. Cheap public transport increases the opportunities for employment and access to key services for people who cannot afford to own and run a car.

The extent to which these objectives are realized is to some extent measurable. Regarding viability of the services, the trend over the years for bus services to be cut back following reduced custom as fares have been raised has produced a vicious circle of decline. In London, for example, between 1970 and 1980 there was a fall of 36 per cent in bus travel and 17 per cent on the Underground. While some of this reduction was due to such factors as the fall in population and in employment, the calculation is that 9 per cent of the fall in bus travel and 7 per cent of the fall in tube travel was attributable to rises in the real cost of fares and resulting falls in service levels (Greater London Council 1982). Lower use of the services affects their productivity and efficiency; if fewer passengers travel and the costs are broadly the same, the services are producing less for the same costs and are less efficient. This situation can only be remedied by reducing the costs, e.g. by closing down stations, branch railway lines and bus services or by reducing their frequency.

Subsidy should have the opposite effect of increasing productivity. For example, capital expenditure which provides for new buses, rolling stock, track and other equipment, should result in reduced running costs. Revenue subsidy which helps to increase the number of passengers will also improve unit costs and productivity. But improved efficiency is not an automatic result of subsidy because the subsidy may not be fully used to lower fares. A study of urban public transport undertakings in thirteen European countries found that there was some 'leakage' of subsidy into higher manning levels and higher unit costs; for every 10 per cent of costs covered by subsidy, 4–8 per cent went into lower fares and improved services but 2–6 per cent was absorbed by higher unit costs (Webster and Bly 1979). Concern about the effect of subsidy on efficiency has been shown in relation to the railways ever since the 1974 Act provided for the financing of a loosely defined PSO. The Select Committee on Nationalised Industries Report (1976–77) stated that the subsidy was a bad one because it was ill-defined, 'not assigned explicitly and preparatory to its disbursement to specific items or purposes' (para. 313). Unlike subsidies to the railways in The Netherlands, France and Sweden it was applied over the whole railway network. Sweden, by way of contrast, made direct payment for specified rail services and rural bus routes. Railway productivity was noted by the select committee to be the lowest in North-West Europe in 1975 in spite of falling manpower. More recently, both British Rail and the report on the South-East services by the Monopolies Commission (1980) have advocated that targets for performance should be set and results monitored to ensure that the subsidized services are run efficiently and that productivity does not suffer.

While the subsidy increases the use, and therefore the viability of public transport services, increased use comes only partly from new patrons. Webster and Bly found that better service levels and lower fares attracted more intensive use of city services by existing users, but were less successful in attracting habitual car users. The GLC calculated that, as a result of the lowering of fares in 1981–82, there was an increase in passenger traffic on London Transport of 8 per cent, but only 10 per cent of the increased journeys came from former car users. Of the increased work journeys, 15 per cent of the bus trips and 30 per cent of the underground trips were switched from car to public transport. However, the effects on road traffic could not be more than a 1–2 per cent reduction in car traffic. Thus the environmental aim of subsidy, to reduce road traffic and congestion, cannot be achieved only through fares subsidy. Restraints on car use, e.g. by restricting parking, are far more effective an instrument, although low public transport fares can undoubtedly help to sugar that particular pill. A longer-term effect of subsidized low fares on public transport was, however, found by Webster and Bly to be a lower rate of growth in the ownership of second cars in households, and this must also affect car use and road traffic.

The social objective of subsidy to public transport is broadly to assist those without cars and the poorest in the community to travel more cheaply and to have greater access to facilities through improved services. But subsidy is not always directed to the poorest; railway travel, especially for longer-distance commuting, is very much more a characteristic of higher- than lower-income groups. Bus travel is more used by lower-income groups, young people and pensioners. The kind of population benefiting also depends on the area covered; a subsidized bus service in a metropolitan city centre, for example, will clearly benefit visitors and well-off shoppers in comparison with a commuter service from the housing areas of an industrial city to its factory estates or local hospital. A third factor is the balance of benefit and tax payment. Most of the subsidy for urban transport undertakings in Britain recently has been met from rate precepts. Not all ratepayers use public transport, and conversely, not all public transport users pay rates. Some users, such as pensioners, pay rates but already have concessionary fares. The incidence of benefit is therefore not always straightforward.

A further consideration is the proper source of finance for subsidy. Should subsidies be calculated and taxes levied to meet them on a national level, or should there be contributions from local communities? In Britain, the railways are largely subsidized by central government, although there is some contribution from local authorities for local services. But bus services have increasingly been sub-

Table 7.2 Estimated expenditure by English councils on public transport 1981/82 £m.

	Capital exp.	Total	Revenue support			Concessionary fares	Subsidy: pence per million bus passengers
			Bus	Rail	Other		
Metropolitan countries							
Merseyside	0.8	27.6	16.2	10.1	1.3	9.2	7.3
South Yorkshire	0.1	42.6	40.8	1.8		10.3	15.6
Tyne and Wear	29.6	24.1	17.0	7.0	0.1	12.3	12.4
West Midlands	1.6	14.1	9.0	5.1		13.9	1.9
West Yorkshire	0.2	28.2	21.1	7.1		7.2	10.6
Greater Manchester	1.1	30.5				12.4	
Total metropolitan counties	33.5	67.1				65.4	8.0*
Greater London Council	100.2	123.5	78.5		45.0	32.2	7.3
39 Shire county councils	7.0	50.3	49.3	0.4	0.6	2.3	
District councils		13.6	13.6			43.8	

Source: CIPFA Highways and Transport Statistics 1981–82 Estimates.
* Refers to five metropolitan counties, excluding Greater Manchester

sidized by local authorities, especially by the metropolitan county councils.

Table 7.2 shows the extent of local authority subsidy to public transport. The six metropolitan counties in 1981/82 estimated to spend £137 m. more than the GLC (£124 m.) and more than twice the thirty-nine shire counties and the district councils put together (£64 m.). With the exception of Tyne and Wear, which was investing in its new metro system (£30 m.), and the GLC (£100 m.), estimated expenditure on capital equipment for public transport was low in relation to revenue support. Looking at the bus service, the expected subsidy per million passengers carried in five metropolitan counties was 8.0 p., with South Yorkshire paying the highest subsidy of 15.6 p and the West Midlands only 1.9 p. By comparison, the GLC had planned to spend a fairly modest 7.3 p. before the Lords' decision.

In large cities in other comparable countries both the proportion of subsidy and the source differs markedly from the British experience. For example, in Rome in 1979, 81 per cent of operating costs were met by subsidy provided by the central government. In Paris where there has been substantial investment in new lines, coaches and stations, the proportion was 56 per cent. The subsidy is met from the tax revenue of both central and local government roughly in the proportion of two-thirds to one-third, and from a special payroll tax ('versement transport') levied on employers within the city. West German cities are able to draw on federal and provincial tax revenue for subsidy; Hamburg got 33 per cent of its costs from subsidy and Munich 48 per cent. Seventy-two per cent subsidy for Rotterdam and New York, 57 per cent for Stockholm, 62 per cent for Barcelona – the list in 1979 continues with London the lowest at 25 per cent. Following the sharp reduction in fares in London in 1981, the proportion rose to 46 per cent, but the sudden reversal in 1982 and raising of fares by 100 per cent following the Lords' decision dropped the proportion back to approximately its previous level.

There is no automatic virtue in subsidy, nor is there any in withholding it. What matters is whether the system is able to provide the viable and efficient service which a large city requires to service its needs, and its poorer citizens are able to afford. In the period immediately following the 100 per cent fares rise in London in 1982, bus and tube usage dropped by 20 per cent and 12 per cent respectively, and road traffic increased by 2 per cent accompanied by increases in cycle and motor-cycle use. Productivity on both buses and Underground fell because of the fall in passenger loading in relation to fixed costs. Reduction in service frequencies followed in an attempt to effect savings in expenditure. At the same time, greater road traffic and congestion increased operation costs for buses. In these circumstances the cycle of decline could continue and will probably settle at the level where demand is most inelastic, i.e. where the need to travel is greater and the option and cost of alternative methods of travel are both more expensive and time-consuming than the high cost of public transport. But there may well be longer-term consequences. Firms in London will have trouble recruiting employees because of high travel costs, just as unemployment within London will increase because many people will not be able to afford to travel to work. Shops and entertainments in the centre will suffer and the decline of central London may set in. That would be a heavy price to pay for 'fiduciary duty', as laid down in the Law Lords' judgment.

Any solution for London must include three important factors. First, it must be recognized that the servicing of a capital city requires an adequate passenger transport system and that will require adequate investment and substantial subsidy. Second, it is unreasonable to expect the subsidy to come solely from London's businesses and citizens, since there is considerable use of the network by visitors from outside London and, indeed, Britain. Therefore there has to be a contribution from national taxation. Third, London's transport network cannot be given rational consideration while it is split between London Transport and British Rail. There needs to be co-ordination of investment, operations and fares structure. This can be achieved either by setting up a new co-ordinating authority along the lines suggested by Peter Masefield or the Commons Select Committee on Transport (modelled on German experience) or, as the GLC suggested in 1976, by allowing the GLC to buy-in British Rail services. Either solution will require new legislation. Meanwhile the struggle between the government and the GLC entered a new phase as the GLC took steps in November 1982, following the consideration of a plan for transport, to reduce fares again in 1983 with the support of fresh legal advice, while the government introduced its Transport Bill which authorized the Secretary of State to set guidelines for local authority subsidies. A further determination of the conflict in the courts could be the outcome.

The London problem is both complex and acute and will be solved only when political tempers have cooled. In the metropolitan counties, the legal challenge to subsidy was staved off because it was operated under a different Act, but the new Transport Bill would apply to them equally. The Conservative government is likely to mount all the pressure it can on the county councils when the Bill become law. Concessionary fares for pensioners are, however, exempt from the conflict and have been accepted. In the country areas the situation is less dramatic but more chronic. Country bus services are likely to continue their decline and further pressure on British Railways may cause the closure of more sparsely used lines. Shire county councils have been slow to provide subsidy and most will need little encouragement to withdraw it. Car ownership is therefore likely to increase further, with greater deprivation still for the households who cannot afford them. The rural problem needs to be tackled through the identification of minimum service networks and the application of specific subsidies to them, both on bus and rail.

The hidden subsidy to private cars

The dispute over subsidized public transport has been marked by maximum publicity and political controversy. In complete contrast, the larger subsidy to private motorists is little known, rarely mentioned and, to date, has not been effectively challenged politically. This 'hidden' subsidy is provided by certain tax reliefs and allowances to private car owners and users. The purchase of cars by companies for their higher-paid employees is a widespread practice, frequently designed to provide a fringe benefit and thus enable the employee to avoid paying for the car out of personal taxed income. As such, it can be described as a method of tax avoidance which has been estimated as a cost to the Exchequer of at least £1,000 m. per annum (Potter 1981). An analysis of new-car purchases made in 1980 showed that 46 per cent of new cars were bought by companies which registered them in the companies' name, but if to that proportion is added the cars bought by companies but registered in the name of an employee, it rises to a figure in the range of 55–65 per cent (Potter 1980). It is likely that company financed cars now account for 10–15 per cent of the total car stock. About two-thirds of the total amount spent by companies on car purchase are for fringe benefit purposes, and three-quarters of the running costs of company cars are paid for by the firms. One estimate of the extent of subsidy is that 12 per cent of all car mileage performed and 17 per cent of car mileage for commuting is subsidized through company car purchase (Plowden 1980). This does not include mileage expenses for business trips which are acknowledged to contain an element of subsidy. The total cost of all these subsidies is estimated at over £2,500 m. per annum. The benefit of the subsidy goes preponderantly to the better-off socio-economic groups: 45 per cent of those receiving subsidized vehicles in 1975–76 were from professional and employer socio-economic households who represented 19 per cent of all households. Although these subsidies to the private car from tax payers have to be balanced against annual tax contributions for excise duty and fuel, on balance it is likely that the net subsidy to private motoring well exceeds the subsidies to public passenger transport. But the massive nature of this subsidy is not shown in public expenditure accounts and is rarely mentioned in the public debates on the subject, which invariably centre on contributions made by tax and ratepayers to the public transport services. Moreover, by subsidizing car use, the hidden subsidy distorts the individual's perception of the relative costs of travel by car or public transport and artificially cheapens the cost of car travel. This distorts the real competitive position in exactly the same way as the subsidized bus or train ticket.

Governments have proved reluctant to remove the subsidy that car users receive. The Department of the Environment Transport Consultation Document (1976) said that the government would not lightly contemplate proposals which would lead, over time, to increases in cost, but it argued that there was a need for 'a system which is fair as between transport users and, in the urban areas, gives public transport a better chance to do its job' (para. 5.15). Proposals to tax car and fuel benefits through PAYE have not to date been brought into practice. In 1981, the Inland Revenue decided to defer their proposed draft regulations after discussions had taken place with relevant parties and organizations. One possible reason for the failure to act is the importance of company car purchases to the British motor vehicle industry. In 1975, 40 per cent of all British cars were sold to companies, including car hire fleet firms, and although companies may recently be turning more to imported cars, it is likely that the proportion is still of substantial importance to the British car industry. The other reason for inaction must remain the considerable unpopularity of a move which would raise private transport costs. But the subsidy to motorists should be seen as clearly as the subsidy to public transport and, as it goes to the better-off section of the population, it ought in equity to be less.

One other type of hidden subsidy which should be mentioned is represented by the costs of car and road use met by public funds. While the direct costs of roadbuilding and maintenance in European countries (estimated at 2% of GNP) are reckoned to be covered by tax revenues on motoring, the indirect costs of congestion, accidents, noise and air pollution are a charge on public funds of equivalent or greater cost (4–6% of GNP) which benefit motorized road users (Bouladon 1979).

URBAN TRANSPORT – ALTERNATIVES TO NEW ROADS

Extensive roadbuilding plans in cities, whether or not they were part of the 1963 Buchanan plan proposals for diverting through traffic and creating environmental areas, have been rejected first by public opinion and then by local politicians. But towns and cities have still been left with the problem of traffic congestion caused by the high demand for the use of road space and the limited amount available to meet it. If roadbuilding and 'improvement' is largely out, the alternatives must be to manage the use of existing road space more effectively in the light of acceptable objectives, and to use alternative transport modes. At one extreme, if the most important objective is to permit maximum car use, then policies would in theory have to be directed to clearing roads of all other 'obstructions' (e.g. pedestrian crossings, buses and parked vehicles), setting up morning and evening one way systems to and from the centre for commuters, and building extensive car parks. At the other extreme, if the objective is to give maximum freedom of movement to the pedestrian, the policy would be to eliminate all daytime car traffic from the city area, allowing only buses and small delivery vehicles, with strict speed limits, frequent road crossings and widened pavements. However, local authorities have not seen their policy options in such clear-cut terms. Rather they have struggled to accommodate often conflicting objectives within the physical and financial framework available to them. The two chief alternatives they have considered are various forms of traffic restraint and the most effective use and operation of public transport services.

Traffic restraint

The simplest form of restraint is to ban all vehicles from a part of a town's area, allowing access only to emergency services and delivery vehicles. Such a policy has been adopted for many shopping centres and the centres of historic cities like York, as well as for numerous newly built or remodelled shopping precincts in cities as diverse as Middlesbrough, Coventry, Cambridge and Milton Keynes. It requires the provision of car parking and adequate access by buses to the fringe of the area. Within their limited purposes pedestrian shopping precincts have been a success. But the problems begin as the area and the types of activity increase. A policy which sets out to allow some use of cars within a larger town area has to decide what kind of vehicles, for what purpose and when, as well as what means can be used to achieve and, if necessary, enforce the implementation of the policy. The methods which can be used are the regulation of vehicles by bans and direct controls; indirect control through road pricing and car park pricing, traffic management by systems of one way streets, phased traffic lights and speed limits, plus special controls over lorries such as lorry bans and lorry routes, and special facilities for buses such as bus lanes.

Area control or licensing is intended to control the volume of traffic entering a particular area, usually the town centre. In medieval times when access to walled cities was through a few gates, such control was simple. The alternatives today are either regulating entry via traffic supervision or traffic lights, or issuing licences for people wishing to enter the area which could be checked by traffic wardens or the police. An example of restraint of private vehicles by traffic regulations was the Nottingham 'Traffic Collar Scheme' of 1975 which was designed to control the passage of cars into the central area. Traffic lights on roads entering the city were phased to give only a short 'go' period to motorists while letting buses and service vehicles through at more frequent intervals. The resulting delay was intended to discourage the motorist. If that was the stick, the carrot was a series of car parks on the outside of the area, combined with special bus services into the centre, and a free shoppers' bus on a circular route within the partially pedestrianized centre. The Nottingham 'collar' was abandoned after a year's trial because it did not succeed in deterring car commuters and persuading them to use the buses instead. The failure was due to the too plentiful supply of free off-street car parking within the city, and the inadequate 'storage' space for queuing cars on roads behind the collar which meant that traffic signal timings could not be set at levels which would ensure a high degree of restraint.

Area Licensing is a method which has to be enforced by wardens or the police. It requires owners of vehicles wishing to enter an area to buy and display a special licence. Licensing allows for flexibility: buses, taxis, service vehicles and small vans can be exempt, and large cars or lorries can be charged more than small ones. Licenses can be bought for a day (from a ticket machine) or on a monthly basis. A scheme for 'supplementary licensing' was considered for the central area of London in 1974 but was not adopted, largely because it was argued within the majority Labour Group on the GLC that it would discriminate against the working man's car. However, such a scheme would have a strong deterrent effect on through traffic, which constitutes about one-third of all traffic in central London. It has been estimated that there would be a reduction in the number of cars and light vans by 40 per cent and in car trips to the centre (by commuters, shoppers and visitors on business) by 20 per cent. The saving in travel time reckoned in financial terms would be more than twice the cost of administration (Bayliss 1979).

Area licensing is one form of road pricing which allows the motorist to decide whether to pay the extra cost of entering the controlled zone. Another method of control which can be linked to pricing is allocation of parking facilities. Cars require parking space if their destination is within a town, either as commuters or for shorter visits. The amount of parking space and the price of parking will determine whether they decide to drive in. Parking prohibitions and parking meters regulate on-street parking, and the charges can be varied, e.g. to encourage short-term and discourage long-term parking near shopping centres. They require regular enforcement backed by stiff fines if they are to be fully effective controls. Off-street car parks are more difficult to control. Local authorities can open, close and regulate their own car parks and can regulate off-street car parks open to the public. But they have no powers over private car parks in non-residential premises, many of which were, paradoxically, a condition of earlier local authority planning permissions at the time when unrestrained car use was advocated. The 1977 Transport Policy White Paper proposed to start consultations on the possibility of extending controls to private non-residential parking space, but no further powers have been given. Local authorities can discontinue planning permission for private car parks, but heavy costs of compensation or grants for conversion of the space might result. Powers to tax car parking space might be another solution which would also require new legislation. In the absence of a full-scale road pricing or an area licensing system, local authority powers and ability to restrain traffic is therefore limited.

Improved public transport services

Traffic restraint is designed to control the movement of vehicles, particularly private cars, into town areas, both to improve the town environment and to induce people to use the public transport services instead. The improvement of the services is seen as an important part of this strategy attracting car owners on to public transport by more modern vehicles and coaches, pleasanter stations and bus stops, short and reliable service intervals and cheap fares.

The improvement of public transport services in cities presents many problems. Costly new equipment – buses, rolling stock, signalling, bus stations – and competitive pay and working conditions for staff are all expensive and are likely to require sustained programmes of expenditure. But even when these are forthcoming, there is the problem for buses of traffic congestion so often causing delay and unreliable service. The remedy lies with measures of traffic restraint and reserved bus lanes which have to be instituted by the local authority. The transport operators also need to review their performance and to look into the future with imagination and a willingness to experiment. It is only recently that marketing devices have been adopted by public transport operators to attract more and new clients. More flexibility in planning and revising bus routes to meet new patterns of demand, and the use of less conventional types of vehicles and services all help to create a service responsive to demand. Although 'dial-a-ride' services have been introduced experimentally (e.g. in London in 1974) they tend to be too expensive and fail to attract car owners from their cars. Fixed-route minibuses which may deviate to some extent from their route in response to demand, and which link isolated and low density residential areas to main services have a useful role to play. Such services can be especially useful to the elderly and families without daytime access to cars. By complementing the conventional bus and train routes and acting as feeders for them, the whole public transport service can thrive. Some local authorities in Europe and the USA also have the experience of sponsoring car pools, sharing arrangements, and shared taxis. Taxis are a flexible and well-used service in Britain. A national survey of 1982 found that 18 per cent of the people surveyed had used them at least once in the past month, and the difference was slight between the lowest- and highest-income groups (National Consumer Council 1982). The survey did not analyse the type of use, but it seems likely that the lower-income groups used taxis as a substitute for car ownership.

One important and relatively simple way of improving services is to link trains and buses in a co-ordinated city transport organization with a unified complementary timetable and ticketing service. In the German cities of Hamburg and Munich, for example, there is one public authority (*Verkehrsverbund*) which co-ordinates all rail, bus and train services, whether these are part of the main line railways, or the city bus and tram services. There are common fare levels and structures, and co-ordinated timetables. The *Verkehrsverbund* specifies service levels and distributes government grants to the operators. At key interchange points, often in specially built centres, there are radio controls between the buses and the station centres to ensure that bus and train departures link to each other.

The equivalent organizations in Britain are the six PTEs working under the control of the Metropolitan county councils. The PTEs may run some bus services and conclude operating agreements with others. They are responsible for integrating all public transport services in their areas, and for drawing up plans for public transport development. The PTEs do not, however, have the degree of control and co-ordination in relation to British Rail that is achieved in German cities. In London the situation is even less co-ordinated; the most the GLC can expect is to be informed of changes in British Rail fare and service levels in its area, and it can offer to support individual line services with grants. Through-ticketing arrangements have only recently been instituted. The wide disparities between British Rail and London Transport fares have turned the London travelling public into two nations – those mostly north of the river who use the London Underground and those mainly south of the river who use British Rail. But a request by the GLC in 1977 to be allowed similar powers in relation to British Rail's suburban services was opposed by British Rail and turned down by government.

The most imaginative new initiative in urban public transport recently undertaken in Britain has been the building of the Newcastle metro service for Tyne and Wear PTE. The metro is a modernized and extended light rail service based on British Rail's former suburban lines but electrified and upgraded to high standard, with new stations, bus interchanges and ticketing systems. The cost at 1975 prices was limited to £160 m. By 1981 one-third of the new service had been completed and about 4 m. passenger trips were estimated for the metro for 1980–81. The metro has required substantial capital investment. Its full operating costs and revenues will not be known for several years but it is one happier example in a public transport picture too often dominated by low levels of investment and traditional sectoral practice.

Land use planning

Land use planning is scarcely a short-term management measure, but there is now greater realization that transport needs relate directly to the zoning of residential and industrial areas and to residential densities and that planning must take these factors into account. Low density housing planned a long distance from city centres and industrial zones will, for example, accentuate the need for rail and bus links, but will make it more difficult to run conventional bus services within the area and increase reliance on private cars. By requiring the inclusion of transport in county structure and district plans, attention since 1968 has been drawn to the interrelationship of planning and transport.

RURAL TRANSPORT – SECURING ACCESSIBILITY

The transport problems of many people living in rural areas are grave. Rural de-population, the concentration of shops and services in town centres, cuts in rail and bus services have combined to place the minority of households without car use (under one-third) in serious difficulties. The problems get worse as the population density diminishes and with the degree of social disadvantage. The worse-off groups are probably pensioners living in isolated villages or single-parent families without cars. The rural bus services have steadily declined over the last twenty years and the cross-subsidies which many rural services received from the urban side of their companies' operations were no longer a possibility once those services too ceased to be viable. As early as 1959, the Jack Committee on Rural Bus Services recommended direct financial assistance to the services to alleviate the hardships which would otherwise result. The 1968 Transport Act empowered local authorities to make grants of 50 per cent for rural transport services and the 1978 Act required the shire county councils to produce PTPs which would assess the need for transport and make proposals for subsidies to services. The proportion of transport expenditure planned to be spent on public transport by the shire counties in England between 1976–80 was far lower than for the metropolitan counties. Shire counties planned to spend 1–2 per cent on public transport capital projects and 7–10 per cent on subsidies as against 19–27 per cent and 24–33 per cent respectively by the metropolitan counties (Mackie 1980). The amounts have also been relatively low. The thirty-nine shire counties in 1981/82 planned to spend £49 m. on revenue support for buses against £104 m. for the six metropolitan counties (see Table 7.2, p. 133). Concessionary fare schemes were to cost only £2 m. as against £65 m. As between the shire counties the differences are also considerable, often due to differences in the political composition and views of the councils.

The aim of the PTPs was to get the counties to plan more systematically for their services and especially to lay down the criteria on which revenue grants would be made. The county councils were asked to assess the needs of their populations for transport services and to consult their district and parish councils and transport operators. They were then to produce five-year rolling plans to set objectives, and to sign three-year agreements with their operators to subsidize services which would otherwise disappear. Grants could also be made to assist unconventional services, such as car-sharing and minibus schemes. An analysis of the thirty-nine county councils' plans for 1979/80 showed the difficulties which they had in meeting the suggested requirements (Rigby 1980). The statements of policy were confined to acceptable generalities, and half did not specify, as requested, the minimum levels of needs. Only half the counties had tried to reorganize their services and to co-ordinate them. There were few development plans or attempts to compare the merits of different policies.

Determination of need is not an easy exercise. If assessment moves beyond need 'expressed' through actual demand for services, one alternative is to attempt to establish a universal minimum standard for every community, based on mobility. A more perceptive measurement is accessibility, or the ability to reach a place in order to carry out a chosen activity. Thus motorized mobility is not necessary for a child in a village who can walk to school but is necessary where the school is some miles away. The need will be greater for villagers who lack shopping and other facilities within walking distance than for those who have them near at hand. Accessibility which determines transport will thus depend on the facilities available at a place and the ability of people to reach them. Some county councils have tried to establish minimum service levels as guidelines. Kent Council, for example, had a guideline of a minimum of one or two off-peak services per week from villages to the nearest urban centre; East Sussex specified at least one weekly service within a mile of every village to an urban centre; Bedfordshire had more sophisticated criteria relating the services to the sizes of the communities and the purposes of the journeys (Blowers 1978). Clarification of the measures of 'accessibility' and need will eventually lead to clearer criteria on which rational decisions about the level of subsidy can be based, as well as providing guidance to transport and land use planners.

Grants are not confined to conventional bus services. Since the relaxation of earlier controls on the use of minibuses in 1977 and car sharing arrangements in 1978, local authorities have been encouraged to sponsor and support unconventional transport schemes. A number of experiments with such services, entitled RUTEX, were carried out by central government in four sparsely populated rural areas. The success of these schemes has varied. A study made by the NCC stated that they could be useful, but were a poor subsitute for conventional services and contributed most where conventional service provision was relatively high (National Consumer Council 1978).

Of the unconventional services, the 'hybrid' services have proved useful. Post buses hark back to the mail coaches of the eighteenth century which were allowed to carry passengers. In modern form, they combine letters, parcels and people and have provided a slow but welcome service in sparsely populated areas. Another hybrid service is provided by school buses, where the operators may fill up spare seats with adult passengers. Buses hired for specific purposes are also successful, whether contracted by employers for work journeys or by village communities for shopping trips or outings. 'Community' buses run with voluntary effort require a degree of commitment and a variety of skills which it is not always possible to sustain. 'Social' car schemes are also run by volunteers for specific purposes such as hospital visiting and provide a high degree of flexibility, but again are limited by volunteer commitment.

There is a variety of such services in other countries. Switzerland has experienced great success with post buses. Scandinavian countries use shared taxis with semi-fixed routes in rural areas. In the USA about 22 per cent of car commuters share their rides and the encouragement and organization of sharing arrangements is promoted by employers. Variation and experiment in different localities will no doubt continue and it is unlikely that there will be a uniform system. The county and district councils will, however, need to make a more concerted and consistent effort in order to assist their rural populations if a tolerable degree of accessibility to quite ordinary facilities is to be achieved.

If the problem of transport in the cities is to reconcile motor vehicles with the environment and to maintain public transport systems, in rural areas it is to ensure that a minority of the people have a basic standard of mobility which will enable them to have access to all kinds of essential facilities. In both cases a new class of deprivation can be defined: those who lack adequate transport. It is as much to their needs as to the awareness of environment that transport planning of the future must look.

NOTES

1. Sharp, T. (1970) from Proof of Evidence to the Public Inquiry, City of Oxford Development Plan, quoted in Stanfield (1981), p. 167.
2. Castle, Barbara, Mandarin Power in *Sunday Times* 18.6.1973. London.

Part three
LOOKING TO THE FUTURE

Chapter eight
THE COMING AGENDA

The immediate future for transport in Britain will depend largely on the short-term constraints on capital investment and public expenditure and on government policy in relation to such issues as subsidy to public transport. Against this background, politicians, interest groups, transport operators and government regulatory organizations will co-operate, conflict and interact to produce a series of decisions which will amount, in retrospect, to a policy. But there is also a longer term perspective which has to be reckoned with which may shift the shape of events and arguments out of the present pattern and into a new one. The transport picture is incomplete without an understanding of two further basic factors: the finite nature of energy resources and the impact of new technology.

ENERGY RESOURCES

Industrial society has been built upon the substitution of fossil fuels for human or natural energy forces. As economies specialize and diversify, advanced industrial societies use increasing amounts of transport, both for goods and for people. Transport facilities are heavy spenders of fuel resources and the fastest and most flexible forms of transport for the consumer place the heaviest demand on fuel. In 1978, 22 per cent of the demand for primary fuels came from transport, and over 40 per cent of all petrol used for energy production was used by transport (Hutchinson 1979). Fossil fuel supplies are finite and are being used up at an alarming rate. If our society wishes to sustain its level of mobility and its complex economy, it has to think in terms of conserving the resources which are available, of finding alternatives to them, and of devising transport strategies which use less fuel, both absolutely and in relation to fuel efficiency. To do so, it is necessary to analyse the types of transport used and their relative consumption of fuel.

Of the different transport modes, cars in 1978 used 50 per cent of all transport energy, goods vehicles 24 per cent, buses and taxis 3 per cent, aeroplanes 15 per cent, and rail and water transport 4 per cent each (Baker 1981). In terms of energy use in relation to distances travelled, cars and lorries are the costliest energy spenders on the ground. In 1977, the Advisory Council on Energy Conservation published figures of megajoules (MJ) per passenger kilometre which showed that urban car journeys used 3.1 MJ against 1.6 for commuter train or underground train services and 0.8 for buses. For rural journey, cars used 2.0 against 1.4 MJ for rural buses and 0.1 MJ for inter-city trains. Freight containers moved by road used between 0.4 and 2.4 MJ compared with 0.5–1.6 for rail (Hutchinson 1979).

In terms of outright fuel savings, a switch of traffic away from planes, cars and lorries and towards trains, buses and inland waterways would achieve much, but since the former are the transport modes which have grown so dramatically in the last thirty years at the expense of trains and buses, only fuel famine and much higher fuel prices or compulsion would now serve to effect as dramatic a switch back. However, clearly any measures which increased the use and loading of trains and buses would help to achieve a more energy intensive use of fuel. Thus within cities traffic restraint and car parking restrictions on the one hand, increased car sharing, and investment and subsidy which increased the use of public transport on the other would all, in present circumstances, conserve fuel. Lower speed limits for road vehicles, railway electrification, and more load consolidation and return loads for road haulage would save fuel on the longer country-wide journeys.

In the longer run, economies in energy can be achieved through new and improved technology. One estimate of fuel savings that could be thus achieved is up to 50 per cent for cars and aircraft, 40 per cent for vans and 30 per cent for lorries and railways (Leach 1981). In the case of cars, the largest source of savings is thought to be through improved engineering. Improved engine design could save as much as 20 per cent in energy consumption in a large city and improved vehicle design with lighter vehicles a further 10 per cent. Smaller engines would consume up to 10 per cent less fuel (Hutchinson 1979). For some time past experiments have been proceeding with fuels and power to replace petrol. The best possibility to emerge at present is the battery powered light vehicle, already in use in the form of the homely milk float. Because of the need to recharge the batteries after relatively short distances, the battery vehicle is clearly not a replacement car for all purposes, but it is likely to have a future for city and short-distance domestic use. Cars and other vehicles powered by electricity or hydrogen fuels have not proved to be more energy efficient in comparison with petrol-fuelled internal combustion engines, although the recovery of waste heat by electric vehicles and their lesser need for maintenance are both energy saving in comparison with petrol-driven cars.

A good deal of energy saving could therefore be achieved by governmental policies directed to this end. Higher taxes on large cars, higher fuel taxes, lower speed limits on motorways and long-distance roads, road improvements which reduced traffic congestion in towns, policies of restraint on private cars in town and better facilities for cyclists are among them. In the long run, land use policies which reduce journey distances for essential purposes, telecommunications which substitute for travel, and engine and vehicle design directed to fuel conservation, would be the most fruitful measures.

NEW TECHNOLOGY

Transport modes

Innovation in transport technology has concentrated overwhelmingly on achieving higher speeds. The breaking of speed records and the lowering of journey times has always been an aim and a cause for congratulation, from the relay runners of the ancient world to the sea races of the grain and tea clippers, and from the record-breaking runs of the *Flying Scotsman* to the breaking of the sound barrier. Nor is it solely a facet of human vanity and corporate prestige. The history of transport development shows clearly that consumers will choose to save time on journeys for work and business purposes whenever they can and will therefore shift custom from the slower to the faster mode, as from coaches to rail in the nineteenth century and from rail to air in the twentieth, even when the cost is higher. New technology in the twentieth century has given us larger and faster cars, the advanced passenger train (APT), the hydrofoil and hovercraft, helicopters and Concorde. The uses to which these new feats of engineering can be put are, however, limited. High-speed cars can only be used on motorways and Concorde on inter-continental flights. High-speed technology is of little use in cities or country lanes and of little purpose for short journeys.

There have been many efforts to devise public transport modes with new technology. Advanced ground transport involves the suspension of coaches from overhead concrete tracks by electromagnetic systems plus the use of linear motors. This system is being used for the Maglev project being built as the link between Birmingham Exhibition Centre, the airport and the railway station. The Maglev system is expected to be quiet and comfortable and to require low maintenance costs, although its overhead structures will be visually intrusive. But it is thought to be too expensive a proposition for city transport generally because of the heavy capital costs (House of Commons 1981). The same problem faces the builders of high-speed rail systems; new, straight track and signalling systems require heavy traffic flows to justify the investment. British Rail's APT uses new and complex technology to allow the train to run at high speeds on the existing tracks to overcome this problem. Modifications to the APT are being made as trial runs continue.

Attempts to solve the problems of city traffic congestion by elevating or submerging transport forms have been common. Among the visionary town planners, Le Corbusier's scheme of 1924 projected a triple-level system of roads for goods traffic (submerged), business and domestic traffic (ground level), and fast expressways (elevated). There were also to be underground railways and a city airport (Le Corbusier 1971). Elevated roads and railways, road tunnels and underground railways have been common features of city planning.

Futuristic schemes have rarely been realized because of their cost and the complete refashioning of the city environment that is involved. The virtual destruction of many American city centres to allow for the building of car freeways is possibly the ultimate in this direction. More practical and economical innovation has, however, led to the development of electrical vehicles which are likely to have a future in cities especially as delivery vans, and to improved light or minitrains. New light trains may be developments from railway services in large towns; in Newcastle the new Metro runs lightweight 'super trams' on rail track. Some cities (e.g. Bremen, Munich and Göteborg) have retained and modernized their tram services on the roads as part of their transport systems. In modernized form, trams have the advantage over buses of reserved traffic lanes and higher loading capacity. Such modifications of existing systems clearly have much to offer in terms of cost and minimum disturbance to the environment.

The telecommunications revolution

Far more profound and far-reaching in its effect is the revolution in telecommunications. The technological innovation has two parts. The first concerns the instantaneous electronic transmission of messages and images either through audio or visual means. It has developed from the electric telegraph and the telephone through the telex system to the transmission of television and sound together from one point to another. The second concerns the electronic processing, storage and retrieval of information, which allows data to be computed, filed, banked and retrieved. A combination of these two innovations not only gives individuals at a distance from each other the opportunity to communicate without travelling, but also allows them to find, process, relay and display information to each other. The new telecommunications systems are thus seen as a potential substitute for transport to a very marked extent.

Putting aside a visionary view of lives supported and controlled by electronic devices, it is necessary to make practical estimates of cost, of potential and expressed need, and the trade-off between these and the time and cost that would be taken by the present conventional methods of travelling and meeting. The effectiveness of the different methods for the purposes for which they are intended must also be studied. Human as well as cost factors matter. Obtaining information and shopping by computer mail order may cut out travel but it is of little use to a lonely pensioner who needs social contact and physical exercise. Negotiating an important contract may be less well achieved through the telephone or a telecast conference without the benefit of actual physical presence and the more subtle signals and reactions which can be observed. Nor is the take-up of a technical innovation automatically assured: the 'picture phone' launched in the USA in 1970 was not successful because the introduction of a visual image in one-to-one conversations by phone was not thought to be sufficiently useful to justify the cost.

Fortunately, a wide-ranging multi-disciplinary set of studies and surveys has been carried out in the 1970s in Britain which assesses realistically the likely take-up and use of the new telecommunications systems and the extent to which they will provide a substitute for passenger transport (Williams 1977). Most of the work was carried out for The Post Office and British Telecom and has concentrated on business communications. A key feature of work is the business meeting where two or more people come together to exchange information and ideas, take decisions, negotiate, and resolve conflicts. Until recently the only substitute for a meeting was a grouping of participants around two ends of a telephone. These facilities have now been significantly extended into teleconferencing systems. Small groups of participants may now meet in studios to conduct teleconferences with each other with either audio or audio-visual facilities, so that they can all hear and see each other. Such studios presently exist in five city centres in Britain. There has also been a development of audio conference facilities within offices, to extend telephoning to include more than two location points, and to introduce loudspeaking 'desk top' conference facilities. A further development is the facsimile transmission of documentary texts and diagrams electronically, which can be used both as a source of back-up information and as an adjunct to teleconferencing.

The research studies analysed the purposes for which meetings took place, and how well these purposes were served by the different kinds of contact proposed. They observed that more than half of all meetings were concerned with giving and seeking information and with problem-solving, while negotiation, decision- and policy-making and other purposes occurred far less frequently. They concluded that only a minority of purposes required actual face-to-face contact; these included negotiation, the resolution of conflicts and disciplinary interviews. A majority could equally well be served by teleconferencing, mostly through audio systems only. Assuming that costs were equal, they predicted a maximum potential share of all business meetings of 53 per cent for teleconferencing, of which 45 per cent required audio facilities only, with document reproduction back-up, and 8 per cent additionally required video facilities, while the remaining 47 per cent were predicted to be better achieved by face-to-face contact and therefore require personal attendance at meetings (Tyler, Cartwright and Collins 1977). A further conclusion was that the biggest expansion would be in audio systems built into office organizations, preferably at the desktop level. The potential for video multi-point conference centres existed, but the time and cost of travelling to the studio centres would be compared with the time and cost of travel for face-to-face contacts, and such facilities would only be preferred where distances and travel costs for actual contact were much greater.

Video conferencing is at any rate more expensive than audio conferencing.

Whether these potential markets are actually achieved will depend on a variety of human and external factors. Many business meetings incorporate a personal or social purpose, such as a visit to a major urban centre or another country, so that they may be preferred although the purpose of the business meeting could as well be achieved by other means. The significance of actual meetings should also be taken into account; a person who takes the time and trouble to travel shows the importance that is attached to the mission. An actual visit by a senior person in an organization may in the future confer the same status on the recipient as a hand-written letter. The take-up of teleconferencing is not therefore easily predictable. It could depend on the comparability of experiences, as well as the costs of installation and the relative costs of travelling.

However, substitution for travel is not the total picture. It is likely that increased use of telecommunications will also stimulate travel for both business and social purposes. By increasing the total amount of communication, further demands for communication will be made and some of these will be for face-to-face contact. Travel may thus be stimulated with meetings complementing contact through telecommunications. One study has concluded that the absolute demand for transport could well be increased overall (Reid 1974).

The results for transport provision would come from three effects. First, the substitution of telecommunications for travel is likely to decrease the requirement for business travel and transport provision, even allowing for further stimulation of meetings. Second, the extension of telecommunications to more people's homes is likely to stimulate travel for leisure and social purposes and therefore the demand for transport. The progressive installation of telephones from less than 20 per cent of all households in 1960 to 65 per cent of households in 1980 is of great importance in this respect. Third, the combination of telecommunications and electronic systems of storing, processing and retrieving information could have dramatic effects on office functions, office location and therefore indirectly on transport patterns. If it is possible for such facilities to be provided at decentralized locations, the concentration of departments within an organization in one locality, or of different enterprises within an area, will not be necessary for the purposes of communication. Officeworkers will be able to key-in requests for information to their desktop computers, to process the results and to send them via word processors and electronic transmission directly to other desktop display units. Potentially, this could be done from each individual worker's home, but the cost of installing the equipment does not make it a realistic possibility for most officeworkers in the short- or medium-term future. However, the decentralization of offices into neighbourhood work centres where equipment is concentrated is a more likely development. Such a development would reduce the need for commuting into city centres, lead to considerable decentralization of employment and alter the pattern of demand for transport very significantly.

The implications of the new telecommunications for passenger transport are therefore massive and widespread. They will require the basic rethinking and planning of office work, transport operations and land use planning. But there is little sign that planners have as yet begun to recognize their importance. Telecommunications factors have yet to appear in regional, county or other planning reports, although there was a brief reference to their future relevance in the 1971 Strategic Plan for the South-East. The impact is likely to be far-reaching both in relation to living and working patterns and on the future development of transport systems.

THE FUTURE FOR SELF PROPULSION

Options for the future should not exclude the oldest method of travel which tends to be pushed into the background of transport planning as a 'residual' mode. But walking as a way of getting from one place to another is the one universal mode of transport. It is so obvious that it has until very recently been neglected as an object of study and planning within transport systems. A recent series of studies by Mayer Hillman and others has ensured that it has been brought back into the picture. These show that 35 per cent of all journeys were made on foot in 1975–76, of which the majority (25% of all journeys) were less than one mile. The proportion increases to 51 per cent for children, including 60 per cent of their journeys to school, and 46 per cent for pensioners. Walk journeys are most important in relation to recreation (57%) and shopping (46%), and far less important in relation to journeys to work (19%). Fewer journeys on foot are made by people in the higher-income and socio-economic groups and by those who own and drive cars (Hillman and Whalley 1979).

The outstanding characteristic of walking is its independence of any form of machinery, fossil fuel energy, business or public enterprise operations. The only public capital or revenue expenditure involved concerns the maintenance and lighting of pavements and footways. For the individual, walking is instantly available, cheap, convenient over short distances and, in all except the worst weather and surface conditions, healthy. Its limitations are time and speed over longer distances, and lack of safety in relation to motorized traffic. The usefulness of walking also depends on the degree of access which it provides to shops, parks, schools and places of work. Where these facilities are sited at a distance, walking becomes less useful. The internal logic of the large hospital or shopping complex in a regional centre, or the new secondary school in a town, rules out the easiest access for large groups of people.

Because transport policy since 1945 has overwhelmingly been concerned with motorized transport, less concern has been devoted to pedestrians. The chief problem has been seen as one of safety in relation to cars, and the remedies sought have been limitations on the speed of cars, the licensing of cars and drivers for safety purposes, education in road safety, especially for children, and the segregation of pedestrians and traffic. It was not until 1935 that the 30 mph speed limit was introduced for built-up areas (the overall speed limit of 20 mph set out in the 1903 Act having only been removed in 1930), driving tests were introduced, and pedestrian crossings legislated for. From this time, concern about accidents led to increased sanctions against motorist offenders. The police take the view that motor traffic and pedestrians should be separated for the safety of the latter. The measures which have resulted have been concerned with the regulation of road crossings for pedestrians where there is a substantial flow of traffic by means of light-controlled crossings, pelican crossings, pedestrian right-of-way crossings and central road reservations. On the busiest roads, guard railings keep the pedestrian from putting a foot on to the road, and there may be footbridges over the roads or subways under them to allow pedestrians to cross without impeding the flow of traffic. This provision is designed for pedestrian safety in conditions of heavy traffic but it also has effects on the freedom and convenience of those who walk. The pedestrian is restricted to specified safe road crossings (and in some European countries it is an offence to cross elsewhere) and the facilities themselves may allow only a limited amount of time for crossing; the price of safety is a loss of freedom and convenience, and a more limited access to the places where the pedestrian wants to go.

To improve the pedestrian environment, many local authorities have introduced schemes to prohibit road traffic from town and especially shopping centres. Coventry was one of the first to introduce a traffic-free shopping precinct as part of its rebuilt city centre in the 1950s and its example was followed by many others as town centres were redeveloped in the 1960s and 1970s. Another type of scheme has been to close-off existing shopping streets to traffic, either permanently or on certain days of the week. Norwich led the way with its pedestrianization scheme in 1967 and was followed not only by other cathedral and historic cities like York and Bath, but also by city shopping streets and precincts like Carnaby Street and South Molton Street in London. There are now some 650 pedestrianization schemes in England.

While walking retains its key importance as a way of moving around, cycling has equally suffered a long deterioration in ideal conditions, and has declined in use. Cycling accounted for 3 per cent of all journeys in 1975–76 and 6 per cent of journeys to work, but the distance covered has declined from 19,000 km in 1954 to 5,000 km in 1980, and from 9 to 1 per cent of the total of passenger journeys (see Table 1.1 p. 5). The fall has been much smaller since 1969 and the distance covered rose very slightly from the lowest point in 1973. A principal deterrent to cycling is the danger of accidents: casualties to cyclists per 100 m. miles travelled doubled between 1956–76 (Plowden 1980). An analysis of journeys to work by bicycle in 1966 in twelve areas showed the largest proportion (between one-third and half of the total) in towns where the surfaces were flat and the conditions were safe. The proportion dropped dramatically to under 10 per cent in towns where conditions were dangerous, and where there were hills to be surmounted. The fear of accidents is particularly marked in relation to children. Only 1 per cent of primary and 8 per cent of secondary schoolchildren cycled to school in 1975–76, although a study in 1973 showed that over half the children of primary school age surveyed in five areas owned a bicycle (Hillman, Henderson and Whalley 1973).

The solution to cyclists' safety problems is, as with pedestrians, generally felt to be the segregation of cyclists from fast-moving motorized traffic. The ideal is where separate cycle ways are designed and built into a new town, as in Stevenage where the accident rate is only one-third of the national average. Reserved cycle tracks along each road is another possible solution and a third is the designation of quieter back-streets as cyclists' routes. The joint use of paths reserved to cyclists and pedestrians poses some problems: pedestrians fear the faster cyclist although actual accidents are few. There has been some movement by local authorities recently in the direction of designating and building cycling routes and facilities. For example, Oxford Council's district plan of 1981 had plans for a system of cycle lanes, with priority for cyclists at junctions and improved cycle-parking facilities. It is also experimenting with shared pedestrian and cyclists' routes. The GLC in 1981 planned to devote 1 per cent of its total transport budget to improving conditions for cyclists with a projected network of 1,000 miles of cycle routes. The scope for increasing the proportion of journeys made by bicycle is there. In The Netherlands (both safe and flat) half of all short journeys to work and a fifth of other day journeys were made by bicycle. Some increase from the overall 3 per cent for Britain should be possible at a comparatively low cost.

Walking and cycling appeared only briefly in both the Transport Policy Consultation Document of 1976 and the White Paper on Transport Policy of 1977. In 1978 and 1979 some reference to plans for the future was made in departmental circulars on TPPs addressed to county councils. Consultation papers on policy towards pedestrians and cyclists were promised in 1980, but neither have materialized. What is perceived by government as a non-problem remains unconsidered.

Although the principal initiative in improving conditions for walking and cycling rests with local authorities, there are areas where legislation and police enforcement are crucial to success. The regulation and enforcement of speed limits and parking restrictions, for example, are extremely important in built-up areas. Past experience is not a promising guide for the future. The police do not take a strict attitude towards law enforcement in this area, and traffic wardens are too few to operate effectively. Penalties are comparatively light, and the initial favourable impact of the 'drink and drive' law has passed. The implementation of the provisions of the Road Traffic Act, 1974 forbidding parking on pavements and footways was indefinitely postponed in 1979 because of the shortage of police and the cost of surveying and signposting those pavements which would be exempted; this in spite of the steady increase in the number and proportion of pedestrian casualties on footways, so that they now form one in twelve of all pedestrian casualties (Myerscough 1981).

The scope for improvement of conditions for cyclists and pedestrians lies in land use plans which provide for access and space for them. In the short term, local plans to widen pavements, close roads to traffic, and designate cycle routes can all contribute, and stricter police enforcement of speed and other restrictions is equally important. One basic query concerns the generally accepted remedy of segregating motorized traffic from walkers and cyclists for maximum safety. The Director of Safety at the Department of Transport, for example, has described the total segregation of vehicles and pedestrians as 'the ideal highway environment' (Gerosa 1980). Such a policy accepts and endorses the right of road traffic to go fast and to be free of the care of looking out for slower moving travellers. But if the two are deliberately mingled under careful management and speed restriction, some of the problems of segregation could be safely avoided. For example, a recent Organization for Economic Co-operation and Development report recommended the consideration and extension of car management in residential areas, as practised in the Dutch *woonerf* and German *wohnbereich* areas (OECD 1979). In these schemes there is no designation of footways and carriageways. Pedestrians, cyclists and cars mingle but car speeds are kept very low by the narrowness of the roads, by entrance ramps to the areas and by frequent bends and turns. These residential areas are specially designed and built. Similar mingling may be seen in a much older example, the numerous medieval and Renaissance walled towns of Italy. The shopping and commercial streets are narrow, lack pavements and share both car, cyclist and pedestrian traffic. Lorry deliveries are restricted to the early hours. Are accident rates any higher than in the carefully segregated zones of British cities?

A policy of fostering self-propelled transport would require an important change of emphasis in the plans of both local authorities and the Department of Transport, one which puts less stress on accommodating motorized transport and more on ways of enabling people to gain access to facilities by the simplest possible means. It might also fit into future patterns of transport where commuting is reduced by the substitution of electronic communication and by the need to conserve fuel supplies. Such a scenario is perhaps a futurist vision but it could combine the oldest and newest forms of communicating in harmony.

Chapter nine
POLICIES FOR THE FUTURE

Rapid changes in transport patterns and use since 1945 have created both opportunities and problems for individuals and governments. The opportunities have arisen from the big increase in car ownership and use, the problems from the consequences for the public transport systems and those without cars. The wider effects have been on living patterns, industrial location, land use and the physical environment of cities and the countryside. Government policy, which has an essential role in deciding transport developments, has operated in an atmosphere of great turbulence. No sooner had governments begun to respond to what was perceived as a need to accommodate more road traffic, than they were met with the strong movement to protect the environment and the needs of those who were being put at an increasing disadvantage, both relatively and absolutely, by the new developments. They have also had to decide whether to rationalize or to support the older transport networks of declining use, namely the railways and buses, in a political context which has swung with different governments from advocacy of public to private ownership and from policies of co-ordination to competition.

Early reactions to motor vehicles frequently expressed a sense of liberation and delight. Speed and individual command of mobility and convenience seemed to open up new eras of good living. Roads were perceived as arteries, the life-blood of communities. Travel was a pleasure in itself, opening up new choices and opportunities. Distances were reduced, allowing decentralized living patterns and easy journeys to employment centres. To accommodate the pleasures of the future, the need to build new roads and airports was readily accepted. Almost immediately in the 1960s the counter movement of resistance began. There was, it seemed, a price to pay in environmental terms. The liberating road, so essential for the fast and convenient journey, also cut through the peaceful countryside, divided and destroyed local communities, changed the structure of cities and created unacceptable pressures of traffic congestion, fumes and noise in living and working environments. As the cars and lorries dominated the roads, the public transport systems began to decline, and the people dependent on them to suffer increasing deprivation. Opposition was mounted through the activities of new pressure groups, 'resistance' organizations and some fierce opposition at road and airport inquiries. It was backed by an intellectual challenge to both the premises and the methodology of the dominant transport ideology expressed, for example, in the Report of the Independent Commission on Transport (1974) which put an alternative philosophy and view. The changes in outlook worked their way through to the political level where they tied in with the political response of local councillors to the dilemma of communities with few cars or adequate public transport. Subsidy of public transport has since become a party political conflict and one between the levels of central and local government. Less attention has been paid to long-term developments; energy conservation and the coming impact of telecommunications on transport have barely appeared on the agenda.

Government policy aims in relation to transport were for a considerable period confined to securing the efficient running of the transport industries and settling the ever-vexing question of competition or co-ordination between the different modes. Nationalization of railways, the airlines and road haulage, followed by partial denationalization of the two latter and attempts to co-ordinate them in the terms Herbert Morrison advocated, were the dominant themes in government policy of the 1940s and 1950s. The big road-building programme of the 1960s, launched by Ernest Marples, responded to the growth in car ownership and road haulage. It was matched by the Beeching Report and the cutback of uncommercial railway lines and services. The 1968 Transport Act took the first broader view of the consequences of the recent trends. Its package aimed at a co-ordination of services which would avoid the charge of feather-bedding the railways. Freight was to combine both road and rail in economically appropriate operations, while subsidy for passenger services was to be given for services where need was the criterion, as measured by local transport authorities. Indeed at local government level, co-ordinated policy planning was achieved for land use through the county structure plans from 1968, for all transport expenditure on the different modes through the TPPs from

161

1974, and for public transport services through the PTEs in the conurbations from 1972 and (although belatedly) the PTPs of the shire counties from 1978.

But the framework for co-ordination laid down for local authorities was not achieved by central government. The attempt was made to combine the transport and environment functions through placing both functions in one giant Department of the Environment in 1970 which would then be able to produce co-ordinated plans. It did not succeed partly because the conglomerate department was too large and unwieldy, and partly because of the desire of the transport interests to keep a separate identity. Eventually in 1976 transport regained its departmental identity. What was lost in this failure was a policy which combined straight transport considerations and their advocacy with consideration of environmental and other planning factors. The road builders within the department, who had been given a separate division and regional units in the 1960s in order to push ahead with the achievement of a vast national motorways programme, retained their separate and powerful position. Working closely with trade interests, they maintained the impetus of their programme up to the mid-1970s, with little challenge within the department or government to the rationale for their work. The puncturing of the roadbuilding consensus came from very genuine amateur, grass roots opposition and it was some time before the message got through to the department officials that it had broken down.

The 1976 Transport Consultation Document (Dept of Environment 1976) was the first attempt to take a comprehensive and fundamental view of transport policy. The objectives set out showed the broader range: efficiency of the transport systems, social welfare aims, environmental protection, and the efficient use of scarce resources were clearly laid down as the overall objectives of a co-ordinated transport policy. The 1977 White Paper reiterated the importance of environmental and social aims, which it defined as the need to secure a reasonable level of personal mobility, but replaced efficiency of the services as such by the aim of contributing to economic growth. Both documents made a promising start to a consistent transport policy, placing it firmly in an economic, social and environmental setting. But in 1979, the advent of a new radical Conservative government switched the impetus away from the new consensus which seemed to be emerging and brought an energetic attempt to restore as much private ownership to the services as possible and to allow the maximum competition of market forces between the different enterprises. Social and environmental factors have been relegated to a low priority in deference to the rule of the market. Public expenditure has been cut back, affecting subsidies to public transport and investment in both rail and road. It is not, however, clear whether the cutbacks in investment are solely the result of a general policy of reducing public expenditure in a difficult economic situation which might be lifted in the future in favour of a resumption of a higher level of roadbuilding. Recent emphasis in the White Paper on Roads of 1980 on priority for roads which aid economic recovery and development suggests that the springboard has been set in position for future take-off when expenditure controls are less stringent.

If, however, we take the objectives of the 1976 consultation document, some attempt can be made to assess the way in which government policies have been directed to their achievement. The first is the aim of efficient services which provide facilities at the lowest cost in resource terms. Within the publicly owned transport enterprises there have clearly been attempts to achieve lower costs and higher productivity, to attract more custom and to monitor service performance. British Rail, for example, has in the last few years reduced its manpower, introduced a variety of marketing devices to increase ticket sales and published a consumer's charter with performance indicators. The National Bus Company's market analysis project has set out to identify the demand for different service networks and their commercial viability. These are not the only terms in which efficiency criteria can be described. Government is responsible for a large and essential amount of investment on roads, railways and airports: these are the track and plant of transport enterprises. In deciding where to invest, government should compare and evaluate the economic efficiency of the various proposals between the different modes, using common criteria. The need to do so has been consistently acknowledged by government since 1967 and was reiterated in 1976 and in the Leitch Report (1977), but there are persistent criticisms that the objective is not achieved. D. N. M. Starkie, for example, points out that while trunk road proposals are assessed on a modified cost benefit analysis basis, inter-city rail investment is judged on a financial appraisal related to the extra revenue generated and/or a reduction in costs (Starkie 1979). Local authorities do not use common economic criteria when they decide how much to invest on new buses or new roads or to spend on revenue subsidy or road maintenance. In London, the GLC assesses road schemes on a points system it has devised and

London Transport investment on the basis of the passenger miles generated per pound invested, but certain more complex trunk road schemes and major London Transport proposals are appraised additionally through cost benefit analysis. The political need to make an equitable distribution of resources between regions or areas may also influence grant and investment decisions. The Humber Bridge is a notorious example of a politically influenced decision, but the arguments put forward in the 1977 White Paper that link transport investment to growth frequently point in the same direction because of the desire to aid the regions of high unemployment. Transport Policies and Programmes for the counties are not decided on economic criteria in any systematic way.

The assumption that new roads engender economic growth has been challenged by several sources. The Leitch Report (1977: App. G) pointed out that transport costs were a low proportion of most industries' costs and that a reduction in transport costs was far less significant to a firm than, for example, savings in labour costs. Moreover, improved roads could lead as readily to the import of goods into an area as to the manufacture and export of goods from it. Nor did the evidence point to the importance of new or improved roads as an important factor in decisions on the location of new industries. It concluded that improvements to the trunk road system would have only a limited effect on industrial location and growth except where new roads linked previously separated regions. Other studies bear out these arguments. For example, the M25 road proposals have been assessed as likely to be helpful to the efficiency of industry, but of far less importance in creating growth than a general upturn in demand (Vickerman 1980). A study by the GLC suggested that motorway access and good local roads were less important factors in influencing firms to locate in London than the strength of the London market, the retention of staff and adequate sites (Howard 1980). Government policy nevertheless continues to stress the benefits of new roads to economic recovery and development. The 1980 White Paper on Roads justified its roadbuilding proposals in the context of their contribution to national economic recovery. Its first priority was for roads which it was thought would remove restraints on industrial development by attracting new firms to replace declining industries, as well as roads providing routes to ports and airports. As an expression of faith the proposals are impressive, but continue to be unsupported by firm evidence.

The second objective of 1976 'to give high priority to the social welfare aspects of transport, and in particular to the public transport needs of those without access to a car' has received much attention in recent years. It has principally been construed as the need to provide sufficient subsidy to enable the public transport operators to provide minimum networks of service at reasonable fare prices and to maintain their viability. The 1977 White Paper, *Transport Policy*, promised 'substantial and continuing commitment to financial support' but added the rider that 'this commitment cannot be open ended (Dept of Transport 1977: para. 14). The level of support has become an important political issue, not only reflecting the hostility of the Conservative government to any general subsidy to fares, but also the reluctance of suburban car owners (as represented by Bromley Council) to pay rates to subsidize the users of public transport. It highlights the constitutional question of the competence of local authorities to take decisions within the powers intended by Parliament. However, the highly visible tussel over public transport subsidy has completely obscured the massive subsidy which goes to private car users in the form of tax relief on company cars and mileage allowances. Since this subsidy probably exceeds the amount which goes to public transport and since it largely benefits the most prosperous economic groups in managerial and professional positions, it should clearly be a social objective of high priority to end an unjustified handout to the most advantaged. To add to the benefits of car ownership a bonus of financial subsidy is manifestly inequitable in social terms.

But social objectives should not be confined to consideration of public transport. The real problem of those without cars is that they may lack access to facilities. Other remedies can be to ensure that public facilities such as schools and hospitals are not concentrated in regional centres which require long journeys by cars, and cannot readily be reached by bus or train. Planning regulations and schemes can ensure that provision for shops is made in local centres. Cycle lanes and facilities, and pedestrian routes can facilitate access to all facilities and should be as much a part of social consideration in planning as buses and trains.

The third objective 'to protect and relieve the community from the unwarranted impact of transport on the environment' covers a wide range of possible policies. Certainly the building of new roads, airports and other transport facilities may have an unwelcome impact and protests against them will continue to be vocal for all except the by-passes which bring clear environmental gains. There will no doubt be a continuing struggle between the advocates of new facilities on economic grounds and the objectors who argue the environmental case and seek to refute the economic one. The conflict between national gain and the local cost, clearly seen in the airports struggle, has no equitable solution. When all the assessments have been made, the decisions will be taken on a trial of political pressure and strength. But good environment is not only a question of stopping new roads and airports. In the cities the right mix of policies is a more complex one. Subsidies which keep a good network of public transport in being will help to keep traffic congestion down, but will not on their own induce car owners to leave their cars at home. Restraints on vehicle use have to be added. The control of car parking is probably the single most important measure in preventing car commuting. Unfortunately it is not within the overall power of local authorities because, although they can control on-street and public car parking, they lack powers to control private car parks. Area licensing schemes are an important further method of regulating traffic since they extend to lorry and through traffic as well as to private vehicles, and there are other refinements of 'collar' schemes and phased traffic lights which can be used. A third essential factor is the ability and readiness of the police to enforce the law on parking offences. With some combination of such measures, a proper degree of control can be kept of motorized traffic where the will to do so exists.

The volume of motor traffic is not the only measurement of poor environment. The impact of different types of traffic is also important. In particular, large lorries cause the greatest perceived disturbance because of their size, weight and noise and threat to pedestrian safety. The growth in the number of very large 'juggernaut' lorries is likely to continue as a trade preference but the real struggle has been over the increase of permitted lorry weights. The government has promised a series of remedial measures, including proposals for road by-passes to towns and villages, local lorry control schemes and reductions in lorry noise levels. But these are to follow in the future, in return for an immediate raising of the lorry weight limits to 38 tonnes. Proposals to 'civilize' the heavy lorry by new designs which will reduce noise levels and improve safety standards have been in existence for some time. Permission for increased maximum lorry weights should not have been given until lorries are used which conform to higher environmental standards and the most serious cases of intrusion are dealt with through an adequate number of road by-passes. The inhabitants of towns and villages should not be asked to suffer environmental penalties when the means to secure the remedies exist. The cost of civilizing the heavier lorries which the trade wants should be firmly established and paid before they are imposed on the population.

Whether good environment can only be secured through the segregation of traffic and pedestrians is another question for consideration. It has always been assumed, from the Radburn layout of the 1930s through Police Commissioner Alker Tripp's precinct schemes and Colin Buchanan's environmental areas, that pedestrian safety required segregation from the free flow of motor traffic. While the principle can be held as true for through traffic, there has recently been a questioning of it in relation to the local traffic of towns. A mingling of local traffic, cyclists and pedestrians with low speed limits could maintain safety for those on foot and return to them the slower pace and freedom of the city streets and residential areas that disappeared with the faster traffic flows of segregated roads.

The fourth important objective was 'to secure the efficient use of scarce resources, notably energy'. The 1977 White Paper followed this up by setting the aim of energy conservation through all practical and cost-effective means, with land use and planning policies which decreased dependence on transport. Although it pointed to energy saving through improved engine design and hinted that taxation could be used as a tool to promote energy economy there has been little practical implementation of these proposals. A determined effort to promote energy conservation would intensify research into fuel-saving engines and new fuel sources and encourage the use of fuel-efficient vehicles by differential taxation. It would put a higher tax on petrol, and remove the subsidy for petrol allowances made by companies previously referred to which encourage heavier petrol consumption. Rail and waterborne traffic would be encouraged as fuel saving and public transport in general as against private car, lorry, and air traffic. The biggest encouragement of all would go to bicycles which use no fossil fuel.

Effective transport policy consists of packages of different policies assembled to achieve the desired objectives, using the tools of planning law, traffic regulation, tax and subsidy and public expenditure investment. If policy aims were coherent and consistent, the packages might be as follows. For a strong social set of objectives, there would have to be high public expenditure on public transport, planning regulations and practice which encouraged location of facilities at a local level and good pedestrian and cycle access, the end of the subsidy to company-financed cars, and careful traffic regulation.

Priority for the environment would require expenditure on road by-passes, public transport, and on quieter engines for lorries and cars, and in the longer term the end of private car subsidy and high fuel taxes. If energy conservation was the primary aim, the package would include all the social objective measures plus the development through public expenditure of rail and water transport, more energy-efficient vehicle engines and an encouragement of telecommunications use where it saved journeys. Emphasis on meeting the directly expressed needs of industry would include in its package high investment in roads, heavier lorry weights and low fuel tax, but a policy which aimed to secure the most efficient allocation of economic resources would modify these demands and would require industry to meet its true cost through higher vehicle and fuel taxation. It would also judge investment and pricing proposals on clear common economic criteria.

The reality of political life and governmental planning is unlikely in the future, as it has been in the past, to allow such 'rational' policy packages to be assembled. Party policies and the pressure of client and consumer groups in practice decide the mix. The present absolute requirement of the Conservative government of 1979 for low public expenditure overrides a more usual commitment to policies of roadbuilding as well as cutting back on both capital expenditure and revenue subsidy for the public transport operators. A more moderate and conventional policy would allow the mitigation of these policies with higher public expenditure both on roads and public transport. Labour policy, traditionally influenced by the transport unions, would direct more expenditure into rail and public transport. Pressure from residents' groups against new roads, often well organized by middle-class communities, is often effective, but the same groups are unlikely to support higher fuel taxes or the removal of subsidy to company cars which are part of an 'environment' package. In a political struggle for the share-out of public goods, the best-placed to succeed are the producer groups, i.e. the established roads and industry lobbies on the one hand and the trade union-backed public transport and rail lobby on the other. At local level, the Labour councillors' groups pushing to secure adequate local public transport and the local residents' groups campaigning against specific road proposals also do well. The causes without strong interest group backing, such as conservationists intent on saving energy resources, are unlikely to achieve their aims until they can harness voter or interest group power. Above all, the public desire to own and use cars at the lowest cost will inhibit governments from unpopular moves to secure effective controls over their use and see that they pay the true costs of their transport mode.

The ideal transport policy may be hard to achieve in the irreconcilability of inconsistent aims and the pull of counter pressures. Nevertheless, there are two aims worth keeping in mind as a guide in the future. One is to secure access for all people to the goods and services that they need through transport means, and the other is to see that in so doing they do not destroy the environment and resources of the world in which they live and work. Above all, we need to see transport mobility as an important means to greater welfare and prosperity and not as an end in itself.

REFERENCES AND BIBLIOGRAPHY

ADAMS, J. (1981) Transport Planning – vision and practice, Routledge and Kegan Paul

AUTOMOBILE ASSOCIATION (1976) Memorandum to the Secretary of State for the Environment on the Transport Policy Consultation Document

BAGWELL, P. S. (1974) *The Transport Revolution from 1970*, Batsford

BAGWELL, P. S. (1982) *The Railwaymen*, Vol. II. Allen and Unwin

BAKER, M. (1981) Energy and transport, in D. Bannister and P. Hall (eds) *Transport and Public Policy Planning*, Mansell

BARKER, A. (1979) *Public Participation in Britain – a classified bibliography*, Bedford Square Press

BARTY-KING, H. F. (1980) *The AA:1905–80*, Automobile Association

BAUTZ, J. (1979) Para transit in the U.S., in *Urban Transport and the Environment*, Vol. I, OECD

BAYLISS, D. (1979) Area licensing in London, in *Urban Transport and the Environment*, Vol. II, OECD

BLOWERS, A. (1978) Future rural transport and development policy in R. Creswell, (ed.) *Rural Transport and Country Planning*, Leonard Hill

BLOWERS, A. (1980) *The Limits of Power: the politics of local planning policy*, Pergamon

BLUNKETT, D. (1982) The road to cheap fares, *Local Government Chronicle*, 23 April 1982

BOULADON, G, (1979) Costs and benefits of motor vehicles, in *Urban Transport and the Environment*, Vol. I, OECD

BRITISH AIRPORTS AUTHORITY (1977–78) *Annual Report*

BRITISH RAILWAYS BOARD (1963) *The Reshaping of British Railways*, (The Beeching Report) HMSO

BRITISH RAILWAYS BOARD (1981a) *Rail Policy*

BRITISH RAILWAYS BOARD (1981b) *The Commuters' Charter*

BRITISH WATERWAYS BOARD (1980) *Annual Report*

BRUTON, M. J. (1980) Public participation, local planning and conflicts of interest, *Policy and Politics*, Vol. VIII, No. 4

BRUTON, M. (1981) Colin Buchanan, in G. E. Cherry (ed.) *Pioneers in British Planning*, Architectural Press

BUCHANAN REPORT (1963) *(Traffic in Towns)* Reports of Steering Group and Working Group, appointed by Minister of Transport, HMSO

BUCHANAN, C. (1958) *Mixed Blessing*, Leonard Hill

BUCHANAN, C. (1971) *Note of Dissent*, Report of the Commission on the Third London Airport, HMSO

BUCHANAN, C. (1972) *The State of Britain*, Faber and Faber

BUCHANAN, M., BURSEY, N., LEWIS, K. and MULLEN, P. (1980) *Transport Planning for Greater London*, Saxon House

BUCHANAN, C. (1981) *No Way to the Airport*, Longman

CENTRAL TRANSPORT CONSULTATIVE COMMITTEE FOR GREAT BRITAIN, *Annual Reports*, 1979, 1980

CHAMBERLAYNE, P. (1978) The politics of participation, *London Journal*, Vol. IV, No. 1

CIVIC TRUST (1982) By-Passes: panacea or pretence?, *Heritage Outlook* Vol. II, No. 1, Jan/Feb 1982

COBURN, T. M., BEESLEY, M. E. and REYNOLDS, D. J. (1960) The London–Birmingham Motorway – traffic or economics, *Road Research Technical Paper No. 46*, HMSO

COLLINS, M. F. and PHAROAH, T. M. (1974) *Transport Organisation in a Great City*, Weidenfeld and Nicolson

CONFEDERATION OF BRITISH INDUSTRY (1981) The Views of the C.B.I. Transport Policy Committee on the Report of the Armitage Committee

COUNCIL FOR THE PROTECTION OF RURAL ENGLAND (1979) *Lorries Versus People and the Environment.*

COURTENAY, G. (1977) *North Yorkshire Structure Plan*, Social and Community Planning Research

CROSLAND, C. A. R. (1956) *The Future of Socialism*, Jonathan Cape

CROSLAND, C. A. R. (1974) *Socialism Now*, Jonathan Cape

CULLINGWORTH, J. B. (1979) *Town and Country Planning in Britain* (7th edn), Allen and Unwin

DEPARTMENT OF THE ENVIRONMENT (1973a) *Greater London Development Plan*, Report of the Panel of Inquiry, Vol. I

DEPARTMENT OF THE ENVIRONMENT (1973b) Circular 104/73

DEPARTMENT OF THE ENVIRONMENT (1976) *Transport Policy: a consultation document*, HMSO

DEPARTMENT OF THE ENVIRONMENT (1975) *Road Traffic and the Environment*, HMSO

DEPARTMENT OF TRADE (1978) *Airports Policy*, Cmnd 7084, HMSO

DEPARTMENT OF TRANSPORT (1977) *Transport Policy*, Cmnd 6836, HMSO

DEPARTMENT OF TRANSPORT (1980) (Armitage Report) *Lorries, People and the Environment*, Cmnd 8439, HMSO

DEPARTMENT OF TRANSPORT (1980) Policy for Roads: England 1980, Cmnd, 7908, HMSO

DEPARTMENT OF TRANSPORT AND HOME OFFICE (1981) *Report of the Interdepartmental Working Party on Road Traffic Law*, HMSO

DEPARTMENT OF TRANSPORT (1983) (Serpell Report) *Railway Finances*, HMSO

DOWSE, R. E. and HUGHES, J. A. (1977) Sporadic interventionists, *Political Studies*, Vol. 25, 1977

DRAPER, P. (1977) *Creation of the Department of the Environment*, Civil Service Studies, No. 4, HMSO

ECOLOGIST (1972) Blue print for survival, in Blowers, A., Hamnet, C., and Jarre, P. (eds) (1974) *The future of Cities*, Hutchinson Educational Ltd

EUROPEAN DOCUMENTATION 1977/6 (1977) *The European Community's environmental policy*

EUROPEAN FILE 5/81 (1981) *A Better Transport Network for Europe*, Commission for the European Communities

FINER, S. (1958) Transport interests and the roads lobby, *Political Quarterly*, Vol. 29, 1958

FOSTER REPORT (1979) *Report of the Independent Committee of Inquiry into Road Haulage Operators Licensing*, HMSO

FOSTER, C. D. and BEESLEY, M. E. (1963) Estimating the social benefit of constructing an underground railway in London, *Journal of the Royal Statistical Society*, Ser.A General

FOWLER, N. (1977) *The Right Track*, Conservative Political Centre

FREIGHT TRANSPORT ASSOCIATION (1979) *Evidence to the Armitage Inquiry into Lorries, People and the Environment*

GARDINER, J. A. (1969) *Traffic and the Police*, Harvard University Press, Cambridge, Mass.

GEROSA, P. (1980) Reducing pedestrian casualties in *Conference on Walking*, 4 June 1980, Policy Studies Institute

GRANT, J. (1977) *The politics of urban transport planning*, Earth Resources Research Ltd

GREATER LONDON COUNCIL (1977a) *Minutes of proceedings*, Vol. 25, January 1977

GREATER LONDON COUNCIL (1977b) *Freight Policy for London*

GREATER LONDON COUNCIL (1980) The impact of Brent Cross, *Reviews and Studies Series*, No. 2

GREATER LONDON COUNCIL (1982) *Fare Levels in London: background information*

GREGORY, R. (1974) The Minister's Line: or the M4 comes to Berkshire, in Kimber and Richardson (eds), (1974a)

GWILLIAM, K. M. and MACKIE, P. J. (1975) *Economics and Transport Policy*, Allen and Unwin

HALL, P. (1977) *The World Cities*, (2nd edn), Weidenfeld and Nicolson

HALL, P. (1980) *Great Planning Disasters*, Weidenfeld and Nicolson

HAMER, M. (1974) *Wheels within Wheels: a study of the road lobby*, Friends of the Earth Ltd

HAMER, M. and POTTER, S. (1979) *Vital Travel Statistics*, Open University

HAMPTON, W. (1970) *Democracy and Community*, Oxford University Press

HILLMAN, M. HENDERSON, C. and WHALLEY, A. (1973) Personal mobility and transport policy, *Political and Economic Planning*

HILLMAN, M. and WHALLEY, A. (1979) *Walking is Transport*, Policy Studies Institute, Table IV: 1

HMSO (1980) *The Government's Expenditure Plans 1981/82 to 1983/84*, Cmnd 8175

HOINVILLE, G. (1977) *The Priority Evaluator Method*, Social Community and Planning Research

HOUSE OF COMMONS (1981a) *First Report from the Transport Committee 1980–81*

HOUSE OF COMMONS (1981b) *Transport Committee* (1980–81), *Third Report* on Advanced Ground Transport.

HOUSE OF COMMONS (1982a) Transport Committee 1981–82, *Transportation in London. Minutes of Evidence*, 3 Feb. 1982

HOUSE OF COMMONS (1982b) Fifth Report from the Transport Committee (1981–82), *Transport in London* Vol. I

HOWARD, B. (1980) Freight transport developments: the implication for planners, *The Planner*, Mar. 1980

HUTCHINSON, D. (1979) Energy conservation and transport, *Greater London Intelligence Journal*, No. 144 1979

ILLICH, I. (1974) *Energy and Equity*, Calder and Boyers

INDEPENDENT COMMISSION ON TRANSPORT (1974) *Changing Directions*, Coronet Books

INLAND WATERWAYS ASSOCIATION (1980) *British Freight Waterways To-day and To-morrow*

JACOBS, J. (1964) *The Death and Life of Great American Cities*, Pelican

JAY, D. (1980) *Change and Fortune: a political record*, Hutchinson

JENKINS, G. (1959) *The Ministry of Transport and Civil Aviation*, Allen and Unwin

JONES, P. HATS: a technique for investigating household decisions, *Environment and Planning* A, Vol. II, 1979

JONES, P. Land use and transport planning – a time of transition, *The Planner*, Mar. 1980

KILVINGTON, R. (1980) Public transport planning, *The Planner*, Mar. 1980

KIMBER, R. and RICHARDSON, J. J. (eds) (1974a) Campaigning for the Environment, Routledge and Kegan Paul

KIMBER, R. and RICHARDSON, J. J. (1974b) The Roskillers: Cublington fights the Airport in *Campaigning for the Environment* Routledge and Kegan Paul

KIMBER, R., RICHARDSON, J. J. and BROOKES, S. K. British government and the transport reform movement, *Political Quarterly*, Vol. 45, 1974 pp. 190–205

LAYFIELD REPORT (1976) *Report of the Committee of Inquiry into Local Government Finance*, Cmnd 6453, HMSO

LEACH, G. (1981) Implications of a low energy strategy for transport, in D. Bannister and P. Hall (eds), *Transport and Public Policy Planning*, Mansell

LE CORBUSIER (1971) (3rd edn) *The City of To-morrow*, Architectural Press, (original publication in French *Urbanisme* (1924) Crés; 1st Eng. edn 1924. J. Rodker

LEITCH REPORT (1977) *Report of the Advisory Committee on Trunk Road Assessment*, HMSO

LEVIN, P. (1979) Highway inquiries: a study in governmental responsiveness, *Public Administration*, Vol. 57, spring 1979

LLOYD WRIGHT, F. (1963) *The Living City*, Mentor Books

LONDON MOTORWAY ACTION GROUP AND LONDON AMENITY AND TRANSPORT ASSOCIATION (1971) *Transport Strategy in London*

MACKIE, P. J. (1980) The new grant system for local transport – the first five years, *Public Administration*, Vol. 59, summer 1980

MARTIN, J. P. and WILSON, G. (1969) *The police: a study in manpower*, Heinemann

MCLAIN, L. (1981) High fares, low fares, no fares, *Financial Times*, 1 Dec. 1981

MISHAN, E. J. (1969) *The Costs of Economic Growth*, Pelican

MONOPOLIES COMMISSION (1980) Report on British Railways Board – London and South East Commuter Services, Cmnd 8046

MORRIS, T. (1976) The highway men, *New Society*, 9 Sept 1976

MORRISON, H. (1933) *Socialisation and Transport*, Constable

MUMFORD, L. (1968) *The Urban Prospect*, Secker and Warburg

MYERSCOUGH, C. (1981) Pavement parking, *Walk*, Vol. III, No. 7, Pedestrian Association

NATIONAL BUS COMPANY (1980) *Annual Report*

NATIONAL CONSUMER COUNCIL (1977) *Priority for Passengers*

NATIONAL CONSUMER COUNCIL (1978) *Rural Rides*

NATIONAL CONSUMER COUNCIL (1982) *Consumer Concern: public transport*

THE NATIONALISED INDUSTRIES (1978) Cmnd 7131, HMSO

NEWMAN, R. (1980) *The Road and Christchurch Meadow*, Oxford Polytechnic. See also: The Relationship between Central and Local Government: a case study of the Oxford inner relief road controversy 1923–74, Ph.D thesis

ORGANIZATION FOR ECONOMIC CO-OPERATION AND DEVELOPMENT (1979) *Urban Transport and the Environment*, Vols I–IV

PAINTER, M. J. (1980a) Policy co-ordination in the Department of the Environment 1970–76, *Public Administration*, Vol. 59

PAINTER, M. J. (1980b) Whitehall and roads: a case study of sectoral politics, *Policy and Politics*, Vol. 8, No. 2

PALLISER, D. M. (1974) Preserving our heritage: the historic city of York, in Kimber and Richardson (eds) (1974a)

PERMAN, D. (1973) *Cublington: a blueprint for resistance*, Bodley Head

PLOWDEN, W. (1971) *The Motor Car and Politics 1896–1970*, The Bodley Head

PLOWDEN, S. (1980) *Taming Traffic*, A. Deutsch

POTTER, S. (1981) *Transport Planning in the Garden Cities*, Open University

POTTER, S. (1981) *Estimates of Tax Avoidance by Corporate Provision of Motoring: a preliminary Analysis*, (unpublished paper)

POTTER, S. (1980) The transport policy implications of corporate financing of motoring. Paper for the motoring costs conference,

Transport Studies Unit, Oxford University, 23 Oct. 1980

PRICE COMMISSION (1978) *The Road Haulage Industry*

RATHERY, A. (1979) Para transit: the European approach, in *Urban Transport and the Environment*, Vol. I, OECD

REID, A. A. L. (1974) The impact of telecommunications innovation on the demand for passenger transportation, Ph.D. thesis, University of London

REPORT OF THE REVIEW OF HIGHWAY INQUIRY PROCEDURES (1979) Cmnd 7113, HMSO

RICHARDSON, J. J. and JORDAN, A. G. (1979) *Governing Under Pressure*, M. Robertson

RIGBY, J. P. (1980) *Public Transport Planning in Shire Counties*, Working Paper No. 46, Oxford Polytechnic

ROSKILL REPORT (1971) *Report of the Commission on the Third London Airport*, HMSO

ROYAL COMMISSION ON LOCAL GOVERNMENT (1969) *Report*, Cmnd 4040, HMSO

ROYAL COMMISSION ON THE POLICE (1962) *Final Report*, Cmnd 1728, HMSO

SELECT COMMITTEE ON NATIONALISED INDUSTRIES Report (1976–77) *The role of British Rail in Public Transport*

SELF, P. (1975) *Econocrats and the Policy Process*, Macmillan

SEWELL, W. R. D. and COPPOCK, J. T. (eds) (1977) *Public Participation in Planning*, Wiley

SHARPE, L. J. (1975a) Innovation in land use planning, in Hayward, J. and Watson, M. (eds) *Planning, Politics and Public Policy*, Cambridge University Press

SHARPE, L. J. (1975b) Instrumental participation and urban government, in J. Griffiths (ed.) *From Policy to Administration*, Allen and Unwin

SKEFFINGTON REPORT (1969) *(People and Planning,) Report of the Committee on Public Participation and Planning*, HMSO

SOCIAL TRENDS (1979) HMSO

STANSFIELD, K. (1981) Thomas Sharp, in G. E. Cherry (ed.), *Pioneers in British Planning*, Architectural Press

STARKIE, D. N. M. (1979) Allocation of investment to inter-urban road and rail, in *Regional Studies*, Vol. 13, No. 3

STARKIE, D. N. M. (1981) The economist's perspective on transport policy, in D. Banister and P. Hall (eds) *Transport and Public Policy Planning*, Mansell

THOMSON, J. M. (1977) The London Motorway Plan, in Sewell and Coppock (eds) *Public Participation in Planning*, Wiley

TRADES UNION CONGRESS (1965) *Transport Policy – a General Council Policy Statement*

TRAFFIC COMMISSIONERS (1980) *Annual Report* 1979–80

TRANSPORT 2000 (1976) *Transport Policy Tomorrow*

TRIPP, H. A. (1942) *Town Planning and Road Traffic*, E. Arnold

TUC-LABOUR PARTY LIAISON COMMITTEE (1982) *Transport Policy*, Report to the 1982 TUC and Labour Party Conference, The Labour Party

TYLER, M., CARTWRIGHT, B. and COLLINS, H. A. (1977) *Interaction between telecommunications and face-to-face contact: prospects for teleconference services*, Long Range Intelligence Bulletin 9, Post Office Telecommunications

TYME, J. (1978) *Motorways Versus Democracy*, Macmillan

VICKERMAN, R. (1980) The effect of the M25 on Inner London. Paper at Conference on the Impact of the M25, British Road Federation

WARDROPER, J. (1981) *Juggernaut*, Temple Smith

WEBB, S. and B. (1963) *The Story of the King's Highway*, F. Cass, (1st edn 1913)

WEBSTER, F. V. and BLY, P. H. (1979) Financing: subsidisation of urban public transport, in *Urban Transport and the Environment*, Vol. I, OECD

WIENER, R. (1976) The Shankhill: power in participation, *The Planner*, May 1976

WILLIAMS, E. (1977) *Research at the Communications Studies Group, 1970–77*, Long Range Research Report 14, British Telecom

WISTRICH, E. (1978) Transport in Greater London: *Political Quarterly*, Vol. 49, No. 1, 1978

INDEX